Sally \

THE GUIDE TO TRADITIONAL LONDON SHOPS

Black Dog Publishing Limited Photography **Brian Benson**

Introduction	**06**
Soho	**12**
Up West	**30**
Old London	**56**
Heading North	**70**
South of the River	**88**
East End	**102**
Westward Bound	**116**

INTRODUCTION

London is a vast, sprawling metropolis; an awe-inspiring fusion of cultures, architectures, sights and sounds. With a population just under eight million and covering 60 square miles, it is the largest city in Europe by quite some way, and is an international hub of finance, travel, politics and the arts. It has 6,128 restaurants, 3,800 pubs, over 40,000 shops, 80 markets, 39 public parks and 147 theatres. To the untrained eye, its physical and social enormity can be overwhelming, but it is undeniably one of the most vibrant and unique cities in the world, and as any Londoner will tell you, it has something to offer everyone.

The easiest way to break London down into more manageable chunks is geographically, which is the way this book is structured. The city is split in two by the River Thames, and centred around a relatively small area made up of the City of London, traditionally the heart of finance, and the City of Westminster, the traditional seat of government. In and around the City of Westminster is what is known as the West End, where much of the entertainment and shopping in London is focussed.

Radiating out from this hub are the 32 boroughs that make up the capital. Essentially London is a collection of small towns and villages that have bled into one another, and whilst it is sometimes difficult to tell exactly where the borders between them lie, each one has its own distinct and inimitable character and community. The elegant squares of Chelsea could never be mistaken for Camden's down and dirty grunge, and Islington's trendy cafe culture is very different to the cafe culture of Clapham or Soho. Each area has its own local shops and venues, usually clustered on what would have once been the village high street, and these establishments reinforce the area's identity. With the homogenisation of the high street, and the fierce competition of chain stores and supermarkets, many of these local shops and cafes' livelihoods are being threatened. As more and more of them close down, the identities of London's neighbourhoods are also at risk. But more about that later. Firstly, a snapshot of the history that lies beneath the London we know today:

The history of London can be traced back almost 2,000 years to when the Romans invaded England in 43 AD, and established their capital, Londinium. The Saxons took over the Romans in the fifth century, and were followed by the Vikings and later the Normans. In the fourteenth century, the city was hit by the bubonic plague, which wiped out half of the capital's population. The situation improved under the Tudor royal family and in the sixteenth century, London became a prosperous city with a bustling trade economy. In 1665 a second plague struck the capital, and the following year, the Great Fire of London claimed 80 per cent of the city. The Great Rebuilding that followed the fire eradicated virtually all remaining evidence of the medieval city and many of the landmarks that define London today date back to that era.

The Georgian period, in the eighteenth and early nineteenth centuries, brought further expansion to the city, and London became the largest centre in Europe for international trade. During this time many of London's finest terraces were built. Alongside this wealth came a massive inflation in population, and poverty was rife. This poverty continued through to Victorian times, despite the booming economy and the ever expanding empire that stretched across the globe. The availability of cheap labour, the wealth of the country and the beginning of the industrial revolution, meant that this period, 1837-1901, brought with it the most impactful period of growth in London's history. All throughout the city, terraces and workers' housing were being built, whilst railways broadened the access to the centre, and sewers improved the hygiene. In shopping terms, this was also the period when much of the London shopping we know now developed. Mass production meant that many goods that had been exclusive were no longer so, and shops sprung up all over the capital, specialising in everything from furniture to art supplies, and department stores such as Selfridges, Harrods and Peter Jones, were established, providing all manner of goods under one roof.

The next defining moment for London's landscape was the Second World War, when the 57 day bombing campaign known as the Blitz reduced huge swathes of the city to rubble, particularly in the East End. The regeneration campaign after the war continued well into the 1970s, and the face of the city gained yet another layer of architecture. London's more recent history has been defined by the artistic influences of the 'swinging 60s', the heavy-handed rule of Margaret Thatcher, and the prosperous and remarkably stable economy of the past decade.

An integral part of London's history has been the waves of immigration that swept the city at various points in time. Throughout the ages, émigré communities such as French Huguenots, Eastern European Jews, Italians, West Indians and Bangladeshis, attracted by the prospects of jobs, freedom and/or wealth, found their way to certain pockets of the city, and made it their home – setting up shops that could supply them with the food and goods of their native countries. Beigel shops in the East End, Italian cafes in Soho and West Indian pasty shops in Notting Hill, all bear witness to the rich diversity that the city is renowned for.

Most of the shops in this book come from the Victorian period and from the first five decades of the twentieth century, with some of the shops bearing a connection to even earlier periods in history. They were set up by people from all backgrounds, to supply everything from coffee to umbrellas. I have divided the book into sections according to area, and supplied a brief history and description of each area. This should provide some context in which to view the shops. They are not just individual phenomena, but residues of the identities and influences that have shaped the city.

In a recent study from the Institute of Grocery Distribution, 2,157 independent shops went out of business or became part of a larger company in 2004, compared with a previous annual average of around 300 a year. The big chain shops that rule the high streets today have a leverage with suppliers that means they can cut their prices, giving them an advantage over small businesses. Supermarkets like Tesco and Asda have started supplying non-food markets such as clothing and electrical goods as well as services such as dry cleaning and photo development. With such powerful competition, the traditional shops that were once so crucial to local inhabitants begin to lose their trade and fade out of existence. Local councils haven't helped the situation much. By upping their rent and endorsing planning decisions hostile to small businesses, some of the city's most famous shopping streets have come under threat, the latest one being the antiques dealers in Portobello Market, who are being forced out by bigger chains with cash to pay.

    As the shops are forced to close, we as consumers find ourselves surrendering our freedom of choice to the mercy of the chains, who decide what we want and how much we'll pay for it. Local economies are damaged as profits drain out of the area to remote corporate headquarters. Specialist knowledge of trained greengrocers, butchers and fishmongers is lost to jaded students behind supermarket 'deli counters', or worse, the frozen food giants. Shops are central to our perception of our surroundings; our sense of where we live and how we provide for ourselves and our families. We need specialist shops and we need the expertise of the people who really care about their premises and the products they sell. Traditional shops deserve to be treated with respect both for their deep rooted connections to history, and by extension to the city's populace.

I became interested in traditional shops when I first moved to Hackney, East London, six years ago. Each day on my way to work I would walk past a Victorian pie and mash shop, drink coffee at Pellicci's, a cafe that has been operating for over 100 years, and buy my meat from the local butchers. I loved the character of these places, the feeling of stepping back in time. As an interior designer, I was fascinated by the bygone fashions embodied in their incredible decor; the nineteenth century countertops, the bentwood chairs of the 1940s, the chrome of the 30s, the Formica of the 50s. During the years I lived in Hackney, I noticed the landscape of the high street changing. Some of the friendly shops I had grown used to were under threat, some of them literally disappearing overnight. My interest became more active and I began to seek out traditional shops all over the city, determined to preserve them – at the very least on paper.

I hope this book provides an alternative view of London. One that gives a sense of what's outside Oxford Street – the idiosyncrasies and timeless appeal of some of the villages. Beside each chapter introduction is an unscaled sketch map that indicates (in a general sense) where the shops are located. It was not possible to include all the shops, or indeed all the areas of London, but I tried to select shops that can be recognised as part of London's heritage; shops that genuinely offer a glimpse of how life used to be for societies in the past. I hope that by creating a snapshot in time of London today, I can inspire readers to search the alleyways and backstreets and discover these treasured traditional shops in London. To buy from them and enjoy them and make sure they stay, still open.

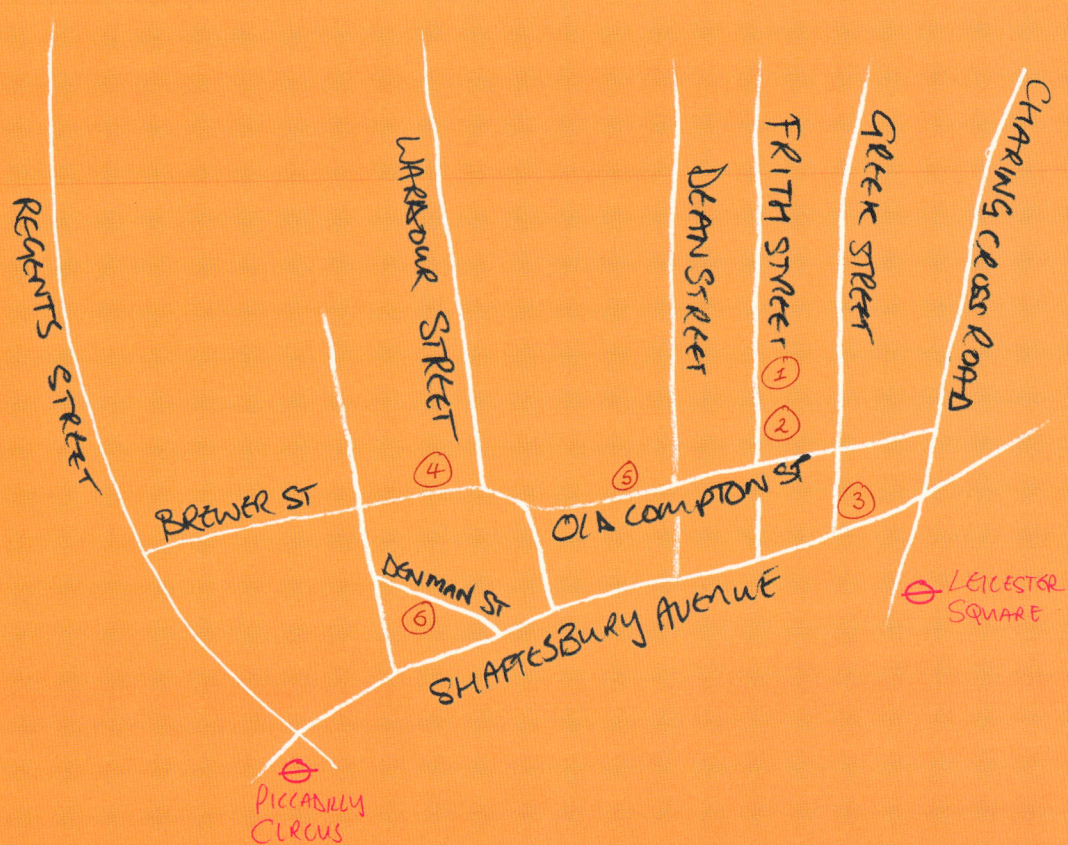

1 Bar Italia
2 A. Angelucci
3 Maison Bertaux
4 Lina Stores
5 Algerian Coffee Stores
6 New Piccadilly Cafe

Soho

Soho constitutes an area less than half a square mile, bordered by Regent Street, Oxford Street, Charing Cross Road and Shaftesbury Avenue. It is a district characterised by a network of lanes and narrow streets crammed full of independent bars, cafes, restaurants and small shops with an unmistakable buzz. This street life and energy makes it, according to some, the heart of London.

During the days of Elizabeth I, Soho was used as a hunting ground, and its name originates from the huntsmen's cry 'So-ho!' In the seventeenth century, the land was developed as new housing for the wealthy, but by the nineteenth century the more affluent Londoners had moved out to the pleasant areas of Mayfair and their homes were taken over by poor immigrants. Soho became densely populated and run down, earning its description in Robert Louis Stevenson's *The Strange Case of Dr Jekyll and Mr Hyde* as a "gin palace, a low French eating house, a shop for the retail of penny numbers and two penny salads, many ragged children huddled in doorways, and women of many different nationalities passing out, key in hand".

During the twentieth century, the area became increasingly cosmopolitan, as more immigrants from around the world gravitated towards it. It was a place caricatured by Galsworthy as "untidy, full of Greeks, Ishmaelites, cats, Italians, tomatoes, restaurants, organs, coloured stuffs, queer names, people looking out of upper windows". The French, Swiss, Italians, Irish and Jews were the main ethnicities to settle in Soho, each group choosing to occupy their own part of the area: the Jews settled around Berwick Street market, the Swiss in Golden Square, the Italians around the streets off Soho Square.

In the 1930s, fascists targeted Soho as a potential recruiting ground and the Italian community was divided in its support or condemnation of the new regime. At the beginning of the Second World War, violence erupted in the streets, crowds smashed windows and in 1940, all the Italians who had been the dominant presence in the area were rounded up and interned.

After the war, many Italians moved back, and still more left their devastated homeland to work on British farms, later joining the earlier immigrants in the city. They brought with them a background in catering and grew to dominate the cafe trade. The evidence of pre and post war Italian influence is still very apparent in Soho, with such establishments as A. Angelucci and Bar Italia still standing, alongside delis such as Lina Stores, doing a bustling trade despite competition from the multinational coffee chains.

Perhaps due to its eclectic mix of people, Soho has always had a somewhat anarchic feel to it, and because of this, a criminal underbelly was ever present. In the early years of the twentieth century, the Italian Sabini brothers ran London's most feared criminal organisation from these streets. Later, during the Second World War, the underworld of Soho was taken over by Billy Hill. In the 1960s the Krays ruled Soho, and in recent decades, the Chinese Triads and the Russian mafia have made their presence felt.

An offshoot of this criminality is the renowned prostitution and porn industry that characterises Soho as one of London's red light districts. In the 1960s and 70s the sex trade threatened to take over the area so completely that the Soho Society launched a campaign to clean up the district, and by the early 1980s all sex shops had to be licensed.

Now we can take Old Compton Street as a typical street of Soho, with its corner shops, peep shows, boutiques and trendy cafes. It is on this street and others nearby that you can find a few remaining shops that have survived the vicissitudes of fashion. An Italian deli huddles near to an Algerian coffee shop, a few doors down from a French patisserie, in a dazzling collage of colours and textures, which bear witness to the area's rich history. Without a doubt a stroll around Soho's somewhat seedy, creative and hip streets will fill you with the spirit that is as alive today as it was in the past.

Bar Italia

22 Frith Street, W1

The Polledri family founded this world famous establishment in 1950, in the building from which John Logie Baird made the world's first demonstration of television in 1926. With its Italian pace, professionalism and sexiness, Bar Italia is a real piece of Italy that somehow found its way into the heart of London, and the hearts of Londoners.

Inside, the walls are covered in boxing memorabilia from throughout the twentieth century, including the original boxing gloves of Rocky Graziano. Two-tone Formica panelling, with huge mirrors above run the length of the wall. 1950s style red vinyl stools are fixed alongside. Behind the raised counter, white shirted baristas churn out espresso after espresso to an eclectic mix of customers. The back wall is taken up by a huge screen for satellite TV transmissions of Italian football games and late-night shows that ensure its place as a stop-over on every self-respecting clubber's itinerary.

A. Angelucci

23b Frith Street, W1

This tiny coffee shop in the heart of Soho was founded in 1934 by Mr Angelucci, and his son has now taken over.

As you walk inside there is a wonderful aroma of freshly ground coffee. On the tatty counter sit an old red grinder and a huge matching set of red enamelled weighing scales once used during the Second World War to weigh out coffee beans for President de Gaulle. They are both in full use today.

The walls are covered in café crème-coloured wood panelling and the windows are tinged with ground coffee dust. The 36 ranges of coffee that this tiny shop stocks are piled up in sacks on the floor. Most of it is sold to cafes in and around Soho, including Bar Italia, two doors up. This place is a real Soho institution.

"STEPPING INTO ANGELUCCI'S FOR MY COFFEE BEANS"
FROM DIRE STRAITS' SONG "WILD WILD WEST END"

Maison Bertaux

28 Greek Street, W1

A little French patisserie and tearoom founded in 1871, this charming Soho institution is a must-see. The proprietor, Michele Wade, runs the place in a warm and friendly manner and creates a cosy, loving atmosphere. The shop window displays a wonderful selection of cakes tempting customers inside. The decor has recently become flamboyant with pink netting strewn across the lamp fittings as if a party is about to start. In its quaint interior, a piano sits in the corner waiting to be played, the counter is centre stage and small round tables and dark polished walnut bentwood chairs are scattered about the room. The style of chair is based on Michael Thonet's 1859 Vienna Café chair, a design that greatly influenced cafes all over Britain.

Behind the counter is a fantastic display of oddments and pictures collected by Michele over the years, and this adds to the tearoom's quirky, nostalgic atmosphere.

All the cakes and pastries are baked on-site in the kitchen on the top floor, and alongside the kitchen is a little rickety room with more seating.

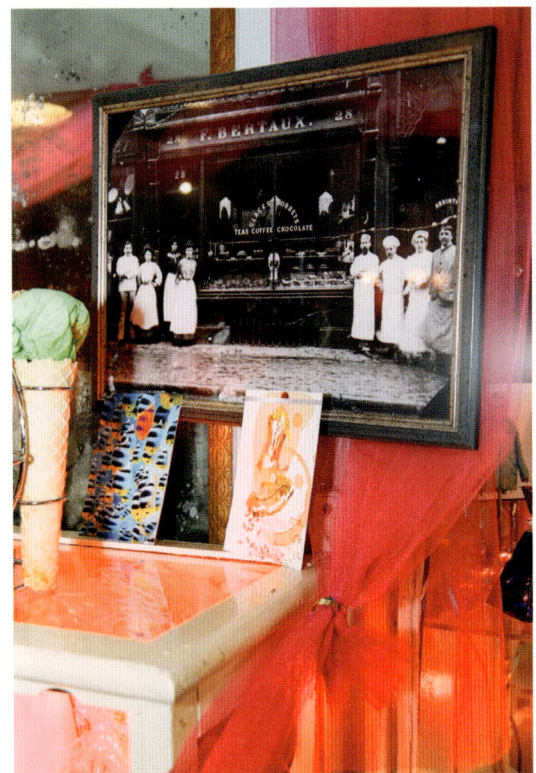

"WE TRY TO BE THOROUGHLY FRENCH HERE"
MICHELE WADE, PROPRIETOR

Lina Stores

18 Brewer Street, W1

With its pistachio-coloured facade and the 1930s lettering, this shop is an unmistakable old-timer. It was first opened around the corner, and relocated to its current site after the Second World War. The Filippi family, from Piacenza, near Milan, bought the shop in 1974, when the original owner (the eponymous Lina) retired, and it is currently run by Tony and Gabriella Filippi, as a family business. They have not altered the decor, and its layout remains as it was in the 40s, with long counters stretching the length of the shop, behind which are shelves stacked high with wonderful Italian delights.

Tony makes fresh pasta on-site daily, and sells it on to restaurants in Soho. The recipe for his popular garlic and wine sausages comes from his hometown in Italy, and was handed down to him by a local butcher when he was ten years old.

The delicatessen is well known and much loved, and is used regularly by television chefs Jamie Oliver and Nigella Lawson.

"CUSTOMERS ARE SO USED TO WALKING UP AND DOWN AISLES THAT THEY WALK ROUND THE BACK OF THE COUNTER AS IF THEY ARE IN A SUPERMARKET!"

GABRIELLA FILIPPI, PROPRIETOR

Algerian Coffee Stores

52 Old Compton Street, W1

One of London's most renowned coffee and tea retailers, Algerian Coffee Stores was established way back in 1887. Having learnt the business from their father and grandfather, Marisa Crocetta and her sister now run the busy shop.

Over 100 types of coffees and 160 teas are sold from great sacks behind the counter. Above them jars of confectionaries and sweets line white painted shelves. Up until recently, coffee was roasted on-site, but new environmental laws put a stop to that. However, the rich smell of coffee still filters out to the pavement whenever the door is left open, enticing customers inside. Much of the passing trade are regulars who remember stories of how things in Soho used to be when Marisa's mother ran the shop, or theatre goers and tourists enjoying the pleasures of English tea. Its popularity has triggered a large wholesale and shipping operation to other countries, primarily Japan, and the sisters run this from the various other rooms in the building.

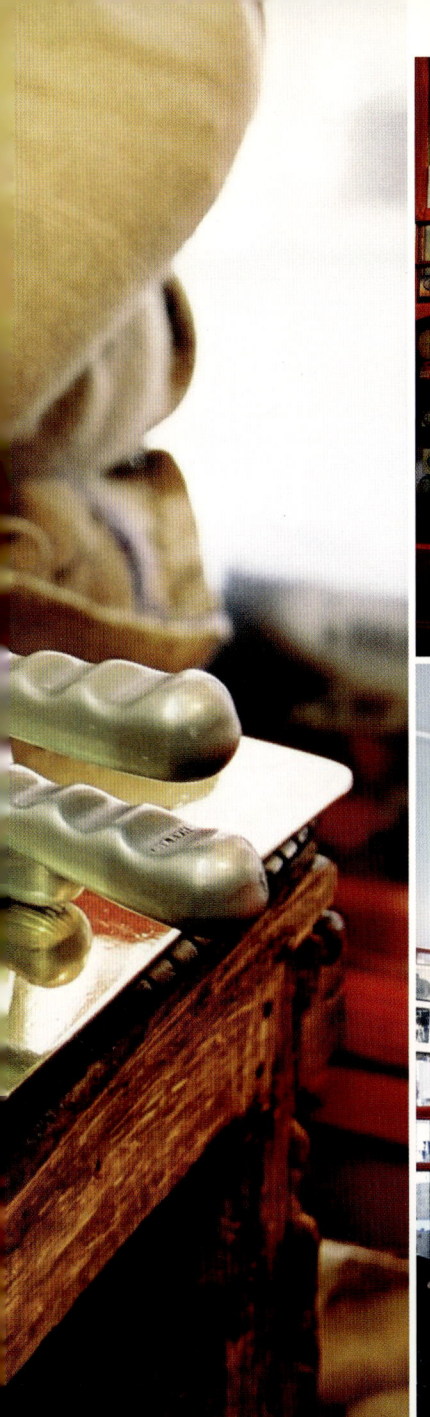

"DONALD SUTHERLAND CAME HERE ONCE AND BOUGHT A TEN CUP TEAPOT THAT WE HAD ON SHOW IN THE WINDOW"

MARISA CROCETTA, PROPRIETOR

New Picadilly Cafe
8 Denham Street, W1

The New Piccadilly is an original 1950s coffee shop, with all fixtures and fittings dating back to that era. From the pink enamel and chrome espresso maker, to the Festival of Britain-era Formica table-tops, the vintage cash register, the neon lights, and the worn booths, everything is exactly as it was half a century ago. Even the menu remains the same… where else could you buy a peach melba and banana split?! The only thing missing is a girl with a beehive wearing an A-line skirt.

The founder, Pietro Marioni, moved to London with his wife shortly after the Second World War and opened the New Piccadilly in 1951 along with six other cafes on this narrow street. When it was first opened it was a rock n' roll hotspot, a place where gangsters and tarts mixed with foreign royal exiles, and where you could buy ravioli and chips for three shillings.

"A GOOD CAFF SHOULD FEEL LIKE AN OLD COMFORTABLE SUIT – YOU PUT IT ON AND IMMEDIATELY FEEL RELAXED"
LORENZO MARIONI, PROPRIETOR

Lorenzo, Pietro's son, who now runs the cafe, started working there at the age of six, washing up and peeling potatoes. Although the other cafes on the street have closed, this one has managed to survive, most likely thanks to Lorenzo's charm, his commitment to informality and his army of loyal diners, immortalised by the wallpaper of postcards from satisfied customers behind the counter.

Marioni says, "a good caff should feel like an old comfortable suit – you put it on and immediately feel relaxed". Film director David Yates agrees and says that the cafe had a "quintessential romantic quality that was perfect" for his film *The Girl in the Cafe*, a love story by Richard Curtis.

New Piccadilly

Italian Coffee shops in Soho

Gina Lollobrigida opened the first Italian coffee shop, the Moka Bar, at 29 Frith Street in Soho. She imported a Gaggia coffee machine, thus introducing espresso and cappuccino into the language and culture of Londoners, and triggering a boom of Italian cafes in Soho. The popularity of these establishments was due to their low prices and lenient credit policy, which attracted artists and students; drinking laws, which banned the sale of alcohol to those under the age of 21, guaranteed a young crowd, looking for a place to hang out. The design of these establishments was influenced by the new ideas introduced during the Festival of Britain, by Americana, which was seeping into British culture, and by the new materials being imported from Scandinavia – Formica and melamine. The popular bright pastel and chrome aesthetic was cutting edge design at the time, and afforded a dramatic departure from post war austerity.

It is said that the 1950s cafe scene in Soho was responsible for breeding the artists, musicians and writers that later brought London into the swinging 60s.

UP WEST

OXFORD STREET
PICCADILLY
ST JAMES'S
MAYFAIR
MARYLEBONE

The areas people most associate with London shopping are those in the 'West End' – the area surrounding Piccadilly Circus, Regent Street, Bond Street and Oxford Street. To the traditional shopper, these areas can initially appear like the quintessence of globalism gone mad. The vast neon signs at Piccadilly scream Coca-Cola and TDK as McDonalds and Burger King fight their eternal battle on either side of the famous fountain. As for Oxford Street, in the words of Virginia Woolf, "there are too many bargains, too many sales, too many goods marked down… the buying and selling is too blatant and raucous". The last remaining independent shop on Oxford Street closed in 2005, leaving the high street brands to claim absolute rule. But if you look closer, and take a few steps off the main drags, a very different view of the area comes into focus.

The development of Oxford Street started in 1739 as a residential area. In the late nineteenth century its character began to change as drapers, furniture stores and shoemakers found their way to the street. These small businesses gave way to department stores in the late nineteenth and early twentieth centuries with John Lewis setting up shop in 1864 and Gordon Selfridge establishing his department store in 1909. New Oxford Street, an extension of Oxford Street, was built in the 1840s to help with the congestion that led into Shaftesbury Avenue. The last remaining shop from this period on this stretch is James Smith & Son's umbrella shop, founded in 1830, which still has an unspoilt Victorian frontage.

The areas surrounding Piccadilly are home to some of the oldest British retailers. The tradition of shopping in Piccadilly began in the seventeenth century when a tailor by the name of Robert Baker made his fortune on the Strand selling 'picadils' – a type of collar then in fashion. He invested his money in the purchase of lands to the north of what is now Piccadilly Circus. Throughout the eighteenth and nineteenth centuries that area became quite gentrified, drawing a number of aristocrats who built their mansions in the area. On the south side, a succession of small, elite shops were built in order to cater to the wealthy residents. Although the area today is far from residential, some of those shops still remain standing.

St James's is the area directly south-west of Piccadilly and it runs from the Circus to Victoria Street and from Haymarket to Whitehall. It was established as a well-heeled area as early as the 1530s, when Henry VIII built his palace on the site of a former leper hospital. St James's palace continues to be used as royal residences, and even today, foreign ambassadors to Britain are known as 'Ambassadors to the Court of St James'.

The best-known shop in this area is probably Fortnum and Mason, renowned for its traditional fine foods, but there are plenty of others. Jermyn Street boasts upmarket cobbler John Lobb at number 6 and traditional cigar shop JJ Fox at number 119, and is (along with Savile Row) the spiritual home of English gentlemen's fashion. The Victorian shop fronts and wood panelled interiors evoke the words of Oscar Wilde: "Gentlemen should either be a work of art or wear a work of art."

Mayfair is an area that neighbours St James's. It has been owned by the Grosvenor family since 1677 and takes its name from the annual fair that used to be held once a year on Shepherd Market. During the eighteenth century, the aristocracy was drawn away from Covent Garden and Soho to the quiet leafiness of Mayfair, and its broad Georgian avenues, elegant squares and peaceful parks have remained indubitably genteel. The shops in this area are some of the most exclusive in London, and it includes Savile Row, as well as New and Old Bond Streets, which house the boutiques of all the great designers, as well as numerous jewellery and antiques shops.

Marylebone meets Mayfair at Oxford Street and is another tranquil, well-heeled enclave, although slightly less exclusive than Mayfair. Until the eighteenth century, the area was relatively rural – surrounded by fields, with a stream called the Tyburn running through it. Its name is derived from that of a fifteenth century church of St Mary by the Tyburn or St Mary a le Bourne.

The area was developed in the eighteenth century by Robert Harley, Earl of Oxford, and the illustrious Portman family (hence the names Harley Street and Portman Square) who laid out the area in a uniform grid of Georgian streets and squares, most of which survive today. By the mid nineteenth century, professional people, especially doctors, moved into the elegant Georgian terraces of Marylebone. Harley Street is still renowned for its expensive private medical practices, much frequented by the glitterati of London.

The area today is still a fashionable address, with interesting shops and restaurants lining the high street. The atmosphere is a far cry from that of Oxford Street, just a five minute walk away.

Bates

21a Jermyn Street, SW1

Bates began supplying hats and caps to discerning gentlemen in 1902 from a shop further down Jermyn Street. They moved to their current location in the 1920s, converting the foyer of the hotel that still exists next door. Throughout the war years, Bates supplied trenchcoats and military hats to the army, using the basement rooms as workshops.

The business was handed down through the family until the last Bates passed away some 20 years ago, and the business was left to his friend, the present owner, Timothy Boucher. Binks, the stray cat, who strolled into the shop in 1921, is still present, stuffed and displayed in a glass cabinet, sporting a cigar and a jaunty top hat.

It is an enchanting shop, rickety and worn with an untouched interior, definitely worth a visit, but do not expect a bargain – the shop has never had a sale in over 100 years!

John Lobb

9 St James's Street, SW1

John Lobb was a Cornish farm boy, who established his shop in London in 1849. His remarkable talent for last and boot-making brought him many awards from the great international exhibitions of Victorian times, and at the turn of the century he received a royal warrant for his elegant work from King Edward VII. Today the company holds three royal warrants from the Queen, the Duke of Edinburgh and the Prince of Wales.

The craft of boot-making was passed down from one generation to the next, and despite the shop being bombed to bits no less than six times during the Second World War, the business managed to survive. The current owner, John Hunter, is the fifth generation of craftsmen to run the shop.

John Lobb has been described by Esquire magazine as "the most beautiful shop in the world", and indeed it does have a very special atmosphere. The shoes and boots are lovingly displayed behind glass cabinets, whilst craftsmen quietly work in the background, stitching leather uppers. If you follow the grand staircase, lined with shoe boxes, down to the basement you will find still more craftsmen working at their benches, and a treasure trove-like storeroom. In and amongst richly bound old accounts books and measuring tapes, you can find the shoe lasts of Frank Sinatra, Robert Maxwell, Jackie Onassis, Lord Oliver, Denis Compton, Paul Getty, Calvin Klein, Rex Harrison, David Niven, Arthur Askley, Queen Victoria and King George V.

37

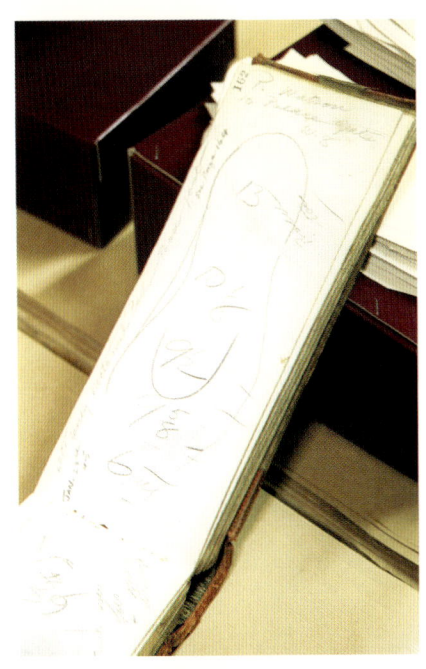

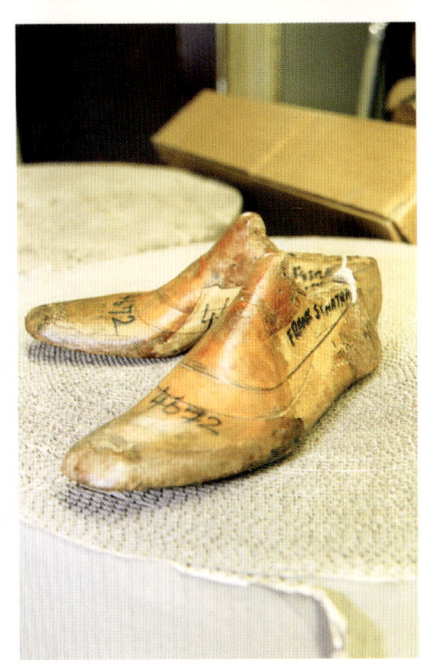

James Lock & Co
6 St James's Street, W1

James Lock was established in 1676, during the reign of Charles II. It is one of the oldest family owned and run businesses in the world and is still London's leading hatters and milliners. Robert Davis first established his business in Bishopsgate but moved to the current premises in 1765. His granddaughter's husband, James Lock, took over the business after Davis's death in 1759, and their descendants continue to run the shop.

Over the centuries, key figures in royalty, the military, politics and the arts have bought hats here. Clientele has included Admiral Lord Nelson, who wore a Lock hat at Trafalgar, Winston Churchill, Oscar Wilde, Sir Lawrence Olivier, General de Gaulle, Salvador Dali, Graham Greene and perhaps most famous of all, Charlie Chaplin, whose bowler hat was invented here in 1850.

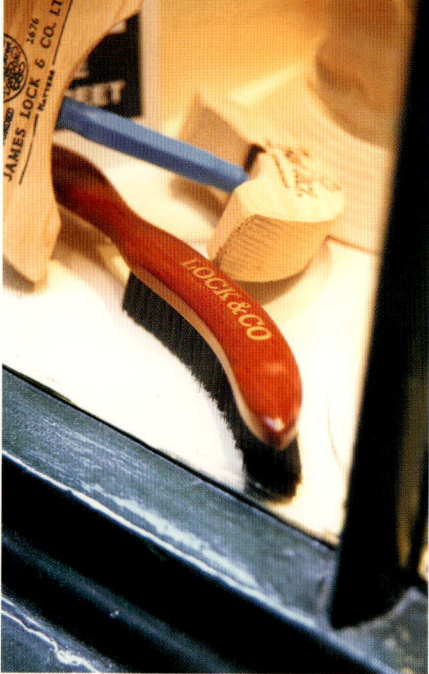

LOCK'S
COUNTRY ROOM

TWEED
CAPS AND HATS
CLOTHING
EQUESTRIAN
HEADWEAR

39

D.R. Harris & Co
29 St James's Street, W1

D.R. Harris & Co is one of London's oldest pharmacies and has been operating in St James's Street for over 200 years. It was opened in 1790 at number 11 by Daniel Rotely Harris, a pharmaceutical chemist, and it specialised in selling lavender water, classic cologne and English flower perfumes to the fashionable quarter of St James's and Mayfair. Being in the heart of the land of gentlemen's clubs, customers have ranged from ambassadors and statesman to field marshals and admirals. Throughout the years the chemist has also served various members of the royal family and of the court of St James. In 1938, it was granted the royal warrant as chemist to Her Majesty the Queen, and in 2002 it received a further royal warrant as chemist to the Prince of Wales.

It moved several times within the same area before finally arriving at its present site at number 29 in 1963. The Victorian interior was faithfully restored, to remind customers of its established credentials. The long shape of the shop provides maximum space to display products along the counters and walls. Glass fronted cabinets show off the fantastic range of products, and the overall effect is rather awe-inspiring.

PLUMB:OXY
POT:BITART:
POT:SULPH:
POT:BISULPH
SEM:RICINI:
BAC:RHAMNI:
PTEROC:LIGN
CORT:SALIC:
SABINÆ
FL:SAMBUC:

Briggs Brothers

5 Ormond Yard, SW1

Philip, the Cypriot owner of this barbershop, moved to London after the war, and set up this shop in 1949. He has now been cutting hair for over 50 years, and says: "I have no intention of retiring, I've just signed another 15 year lease."

He is renowned as a source of local gossip, and it has been said that after having your hair cut by Philip, you feel as though you know all his customers. This is of particular interest, given Philip's clientele, which includes many politicians and members of the House of Lords, the Archbishop of Canterbury, and fashion photographer Mario Testino, who used to get his hair cut here, along with his models prior to a photo shoot.

The shop itself has remained unchanged since it opened. Two worn black leather barbers' chairs, bought in 1957, sit in front of their own wash-basins. Chrome towel steamers, used for wet shaves, hang on the wall alongside black stained wooden cabinets, full of shaving equipment. At the back of the shop there is a red button backed velvet fitted sofa where Philip can relax between clients. He says of his shop: "it's like my flat – very plain, but feels like home."

Barbershops

The term 'barber' originates from the Italian word for beard, barba. There are a few universally recognised markers of a barbershop.

The barber pole: there is some debate about the origin of the barber pole. Some believe that barbers used to fix a pole outside their shop on which to hang bandages to dry. The blood stained bandages and the white clean ones would intertwine with one another when they blew in the wind, and this was later represented in the red and white striped rotating pole. Whilst this may or may not be the case, it is fair to say that the pole was used in the past as a visual symbol to indicate what type of shop it was to the largely illiterate public.

The barber's chair: the classic barber's chair of chrome and black leather has become a design icon. With their heavy mechanics allowing them to be raised, lowered, reclined and rotated 360 degrees, they were built to last a lifetime – and sometimes even more.

The coat hook: this design element of barber shops often goes unnoticed. Early barbershops often have a luggage rack with hooks – similar to the ones you may find on a train carriage. Mid-century barbershops often have a coat stand made of metal or chrome. They are an immediate indicator to a customer as they walk through the door, that they should feel comfortable, and that they will be looked after.

Paul Rothe & Son

35 Marylebone Lane, W1

Paul Rothe opened his delicatessen shortly after arriving from Germany in 1900. When the First World War broke out, Rothe, who had become naturalised in 1906, was called up to serve in the British army and sent to fight his own countrymen. His wife ran the shop until he returned in 1920, and when he died 20 years later, his son, Robert, took over the shop.

Parking restrictions and large cut-price supermarkets proved too much competition for the deli, and in the early 1950s, the business changed its mainstay of retailing to catering. Fixed leatherette seating and Formica tables were installed, and they remain today, along with the tiled floor and the wood panelled ceiling. The shop is now run by Paul Rothe's grandson, and the fourth generation of Rothes is already showing enthusiasm for carrying the business through the twenty-first century.

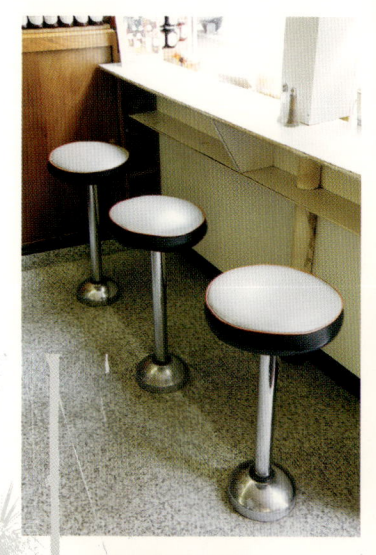

45

Allen & Co

117 Mount Street, W1

This has got to be one of the most impressive butchers to be found in London today. Sitting on the corner of a back street of Mayfair, the architecture of the building is nothing short of magnificent. The interior is equally striking with gloriously tiled walls in warm shades of terracotta, brown, cream and green. Original wooden floorboards add to the sense of antiquity, and a circular chopping block in the centre of the room allows the customer to see exactly what cut of meat they are getting. Overseeing all proceedings is the head of a Highland cow that bridges the door between the backroom and the shop floor.

The shop was established as a butchers 170 years ago by one Edgar Green. Allen & Co took over in 1890, and it has remained as a family business for over 100 years. The shop used to be open-fronted with hanging carcasses outside, but the sash windows are now closed in compliance with today's regulations.

"IT'S A HARD JOB, WE START AT MIDNIGHT, PREPARE THE MEAT THROUGH THE NIGHT SO IT'S READY FOR DELIVERY TO THE RESTAURANTS FIRST THING IN THE MORNING!" **MICHAEL GIGG, EMPLOYEE**

James Taylor & Son

4 Paddington Street, W1

For over 140 years James Taylor & Son have been perfecting the art of shoemaking. The shop and on-site workshops were established in 1857 by James Taylor, who walked to London from his home in Norfolk, to start a business in the fashionable Great Portland Street.

By the late nineteenth century, James Taylor had established himself by supplying the newly opened department stores on Oxford Street, as well as hand crafting shoes for royalty. In 1954, the company moved to its current location in Paddington Street, and since then the shop and the workshops and storerooms beneath it have barely changed.

James Taylor's two sons, and then his two grandsons ran the firm until 1950, when the company merged with the Orthopaedic Footwear Company Ltd under the directorship of Hannes Leo Schweiger. Today his son Peter Schweiger runs the business. He is the fifth generation of his family to produce hand-made shoes.

SHOES MADE & REPAIRED

49

James Smith & Sons

53 New Oxford Street, WC1

"Outside every silver lining is a big black cloud" is the James Smith & Sons' motto, and when it comes to English weather, they're usually right! This shop has an international reputation for making umbrellas, sticks and gentlemen's canes. It was the first company to use metal Fox frames (named after Samuel Fox, who invented the first steel framed umbrella in 1848). In many ways it is the most quintessentially English of the shops in this book.

James Smith founded his shop in 1830 at Foubert Street in London's West End. His son, also James Smith, moved the business to its current premises in 1867, and it has remained in the family ever since.

The shop (a Grade II listed shop, inside and out) is an evocative reminder of the Victorian period. It retains all the original fittings designed and made by master craftsmen employed by the business. The shop front must have resembled many other shop fronts of the period, and is a work of art in itself.

"OUTSIDE EVERY SILVER LINING IS A BIG BLACK CLOUD"
JAMES SMITH & SONS MOTTO

L. Cornelissen & Son

105 Great Russell Street, WC1

Since its establishment in 1855, Cornelissen and Son has been trading as 'artists' colourmen', with an international reputation as specialist suppliers of niche art materials. The shop was originally based at 22 Great Queen Street in Covent Garden. It moved to Great Russell Street in 1987, bringing with it all the original fixtures, fittings and cabinetry. Nicholas Walt, who took over the family business in 1978, says that his customers say it looks just the same but without the gaslights.

The shop is reminiscent of an old apothecary; towering shelves sweep up to the ceiling, lined with glass jars of pigments and pastels. Black painted wooden drawers and antique cabinetry are filled with brushes, papers, gold leaf, pots and tubes of paint. Cornelissen's customers vary from great artists to students but as Nicholas explains, "the more peculiar the request or the more serious the artist, is when our true expertise comes into play".

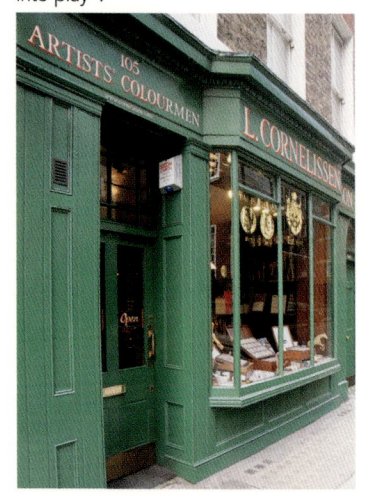

"THE MORE PECULIAR THE REQUEST OR THE MORE SERIOUS THE ARTIST IS WHEN OUR TRUE EXPERTISE COMES INTO PLAY"
NICHOLAS WALT, PROPRIETOR

Arthur Beale

194 Shaftesbury Ave, WC2

Arthur Beale established this yacht chandlers 110 years ago, and the shop is an absolute heaven for all maritime aficionados. With ropes, bells and buoys alongside shackles and bolts of every description, this shop supplies all boating essentials – in a rather surprising location, miles away from the sea, at the top of Neal Street. Down in the basement, a small workshop manufactures the rigging on site. Arthur Beale prides itself on being a specialist shop, and the staff have extensive knowledge of all their wares – as well as being more than willing to help out local theatres in need of rigging.

55

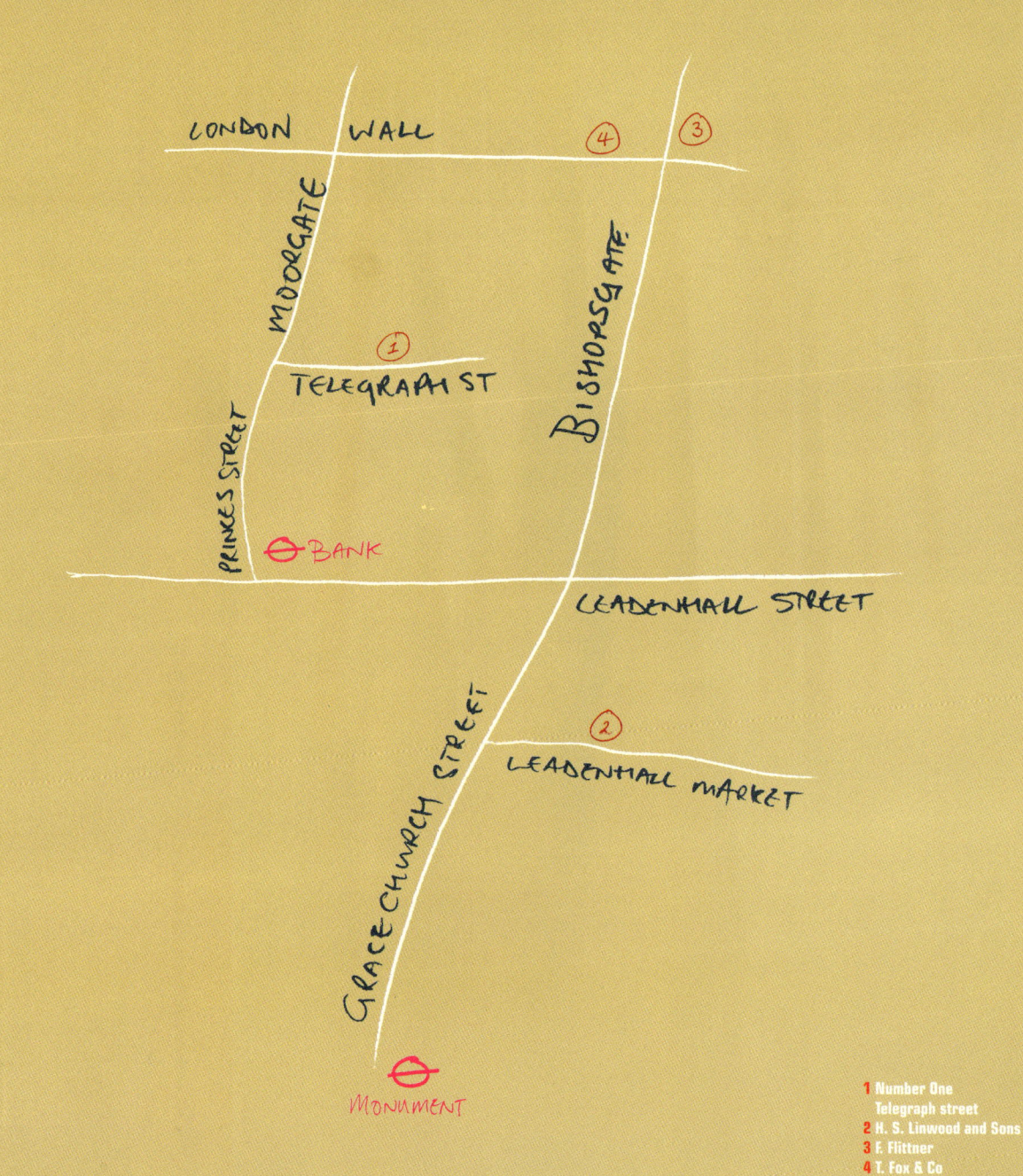

1 **Number One
  Telegraph street**
2 **H. S. Linwood and Sons**
3 **F. Flittner**
4 **T. Fox & Co**

56 | OLD LONDON | INTRODUCTION

OLD LONDON

THE CITY

The City of London, also known as the 'Square Mile', is London's financial district. It stretches to Holborn on one side and borders the East End on the other, and is one of the most deeply historical areas of London. In fact, as it is built on the site of the original walled Roman settlement of Londinium, many regard it as the true heart of the capital.

Londinium was founded in 43 AD as a typical Roman city at a convenient crossing of the Thames. After a failed uprising by the Iceni tribe under Boudica, the city was burned to the ground and rebuilt with a two mile long defensive wall. Sections of this wall still exist, and a number of stations and landmarks around the City are named after the wall's gates: Ludgate, Aldgate, Bishopsgate and Newgate.

From the start, the area lent itself to trade. The Thames is a large tidal river, which made it convenient to get boats in and out, and it was easily defendable.

By the time the Normans took over the city, London was a leading trading port of Western Europe. Food and wine were imported, wool and leather exported. Merchants' guilds were set up to protect the traders, and these guilds and livery companies still exist today, dotted around the City, with the Wax Chandlers' Company dating back to 1358 and the Weavers Company even further to 1130. With trade came money, and in Elizabethan times, the financial significance of the City was formalised with the establishment of the London Stock Exchange, and further, with the formation of the Trading Companies – The East India Trading Company, the Muscovy Company, the Levant Company and the Turkey Company.

The City thrived until 1665, when it was hit by the plague, which claimed 100,000 lives. In 1666 disaster hit again, with the Fire of London. Started in a bakery, the fire spread through the area over the course of five days, consuming seven eighths of the City. Nearly 15,000 homes as well as dozens of churches, the Royal Exchange and other landmarks were destroyed. The rebuilding of the city was entrusted to some of the most talented architects the city has ever known, including Sir Christopher Wren and Nicholas Hawksmoor. Although some of these buildings were destroyed in the blitz, many remain standing and are still some of the most striking buildings in the area. 38 Wren buildings survive, including the magnificent, domed St Paul's Cathedral, which stands proud on the London skyline.

The rest of the architecture in the area is very varied. During the bombings of the Second World War, the City was one of the worst hit areas of London. In a single raid on 29 December 1941, fires broke out across the Square Mile, causing a death toll on that night alone of 1,400. It was dubbed 'the second Fire of London'.

After the war, a rather overzealous regeneration campaign was carried out. With little attempt at conservation, many see this period as producing some of the City's ugliest buildings. It has been said that the Greater London Council, in charge of the regeneration, did more damage to the City than the Luftwaffe. In the 1980s, a further regeneration was embarked upon that continues today. Strikingly modern architecture has sprung up around Liverpool Street, including Sir Richard Rogers Lloyd's building, completed in 1979, and more recently Norman Foster's Swiss Re building (aka The Gherkin). Today, the ancient buildings around Mansion House and Bank seem poles apart from the glass monoliths of Liverpool Street, and yet despite the disparity, the styles sit together quite comfortably, sketching out the rich history of the area.

The City is primarily a corporate centre for business and finance, with very few residential streets. The banks and big firms based in the area attract all the nation's hardest hitters – investment bankers, executives and lawyers, generally termed 'City boys'. At night and on weekends, the area is strangely quiet, with only Liverpool Street station showing any real signs of life. The shops based there are reflective of this reality. Whilst butchers, cafes and delis are hard to come by, a series of high end tailors and barbers have based themselves along the City's side streets, making their livings by keeping the City boys well turned out.

Number One Telegraph Street

1a Telegraph Street, EC2

Tucked away at the end of an alleyway and down a mirror-lined staircase is a fabulous authentic barbershop that has been trading since 1909. Without so much as a proper name to call itself, this really is a little hideaway. The original barber who established the place worked at the shop until his death at the age of 87. The current proprietor, Mr Kyriacou, originally from Cyprus, took over the business in 1970 and he has been working there ever since.

Despite its discreet location, this establishment is still very popular, and every lunch hour brings a rush of City boys in need of a good hair cut or a wet shave.

The interior is well worn; the patched up barber chairs that date back to the late 1930s are tired looking, the mirrors with gilt lettering are starting to blacken and the wording is beginning to fade, but all this adds to the charm of the place. If only the lino flooring could be taken up to reveal the original marble floor.

61

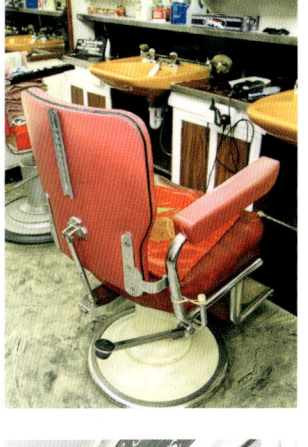

T. Fox

118 London Wall, EC2

This elegant umbrella shop was established by Thomas Fox in 1868, and has been through a number of hands since then. In the early days, there was a hair salon and a tailors also owned by Fox in the same building, and it was common for customers to come, leave their umbrella to be repaired, and have their hair cut upstairs while they were waiting.

The extremely stylish exterior was installed in 1936 and was, at the time, the latest in shop-front design. Curved non-reflective glazing was used for the windows, and the framework was made from black vitrolite and chromed steel. Two prancing silver foxes and a neon sign were the finishing touches. 70 years on, and it still seems achingly cool.

Inside, the shop is fitted with cabinets made of solid Canadian black walnut. The staircase boasts framed mirrors, with original advertising graphics dating back to 1868.

All the way through until 1990, the umbrellas were handmade in the basement workshop to the strictest criteria, and Fox's prides itself on having produced specialist one-off designs for John F Kennedy, a gadget umbrella for a James Bond movie, and umbrellas for John Steed in the *Avengers* series.

63

F. Flittner

86 Moorgate, EC2

This humble looking barber can go almost unnoticed in the hustle and bustle of the city, but once you're through the door, it's like stepping back in time. Traditional barbers' chairs line the room, each with its own marble topped workstation and basin. The etched glass door panels and pendant lights are a tribute to the design aesthetics of the early part of the twentieth century, and still in operation is a payment booth with an opening just large enough for hands to pass through money.

The current owner, Chris Christodoulou, took the business over from his father in 1973, and preserved the original decor, which had been left untouched since the shop's opening in 1904. Chris says the most rewarding thing has been the loyalty of his regular 'City boys'. "Men need to look smart", he says, "but there's a lot more leeway these days. It used to be 'my boss has sent me because my hair's a mess', but now they come because they're more interested in their personal appearance."

Flittner

www.fflittner.com

"MEN NEED TO LOOK SMART, BUT THERE'S A LOT MORE LEEWAY THESE DAYS. IT USED TO BE 'MY BOSS HAS SENT ME BECAUSE MY HAIR'S A MESS', BUT NOW THEY COME BECAUSE

KODAK 160VC
19
KODAK 160VC
18A
19
19A
KODAK 160VC
25
KODAK 160VC
24A
25
25A

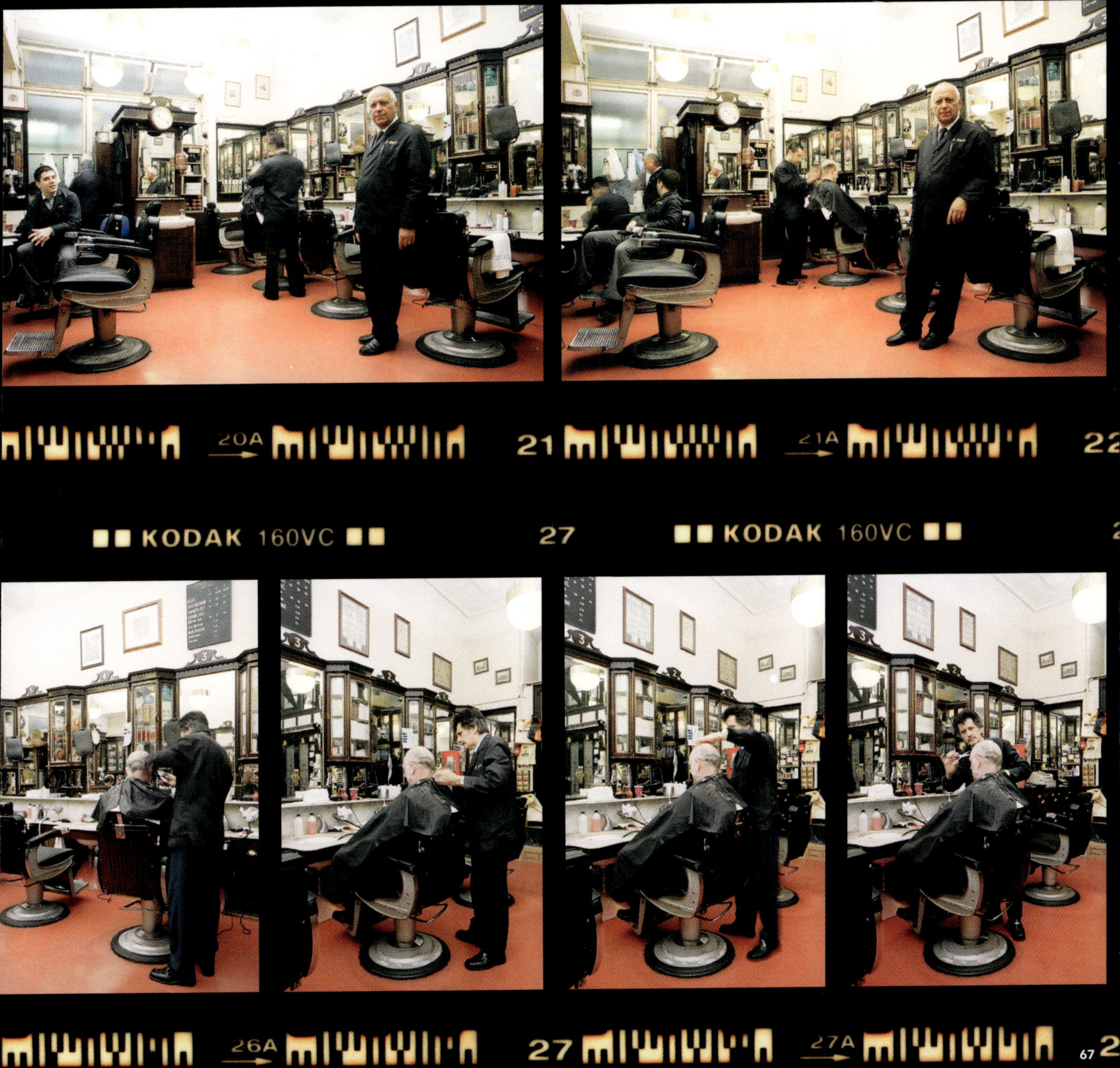
20A
21
21A
22
KODAK 160VC
27
KODAK 160VC
26A
27
27A

H.S. Linwood & Sons

6-7 Leadenhall Market, EC3

H.S. Linwood and Sons have been at their current site since the mid 1980s, and are still trading in the same manner as they did when the business was first established in 1883 in its original location in Edmonton Green, North London. Linwood occupies a site at Leadenhall that has been a traditional fishmongers' stall since the market was opened. Prior to Linwood, John Gow Fishmongers occupied the site for over 40 years, and before them a fishmongers called Wheelers.

The premises are very much how they have always been. The open-fronted stall is one of the few remaining at Leadenhall, and provides a marvellous display of fish and seafood. An old pay station is still in use, although unfortunately, the game hooks on the outside are no longer used due to health and safety regulations.

Leadenhall Market

The first record of a market in this location dates back to 1321, and is noted for trading in meat and fish. The original market hall had a lead roof (hence the name), and was destroyed in the Fire of London in 1666. The present structure was rebuilt by the architect Sir Horace Jones, in 1881. He enlarged the market to sell leather and wool, basing his designs on medieval streets; cobbled and intertwining avenues lined with stalls. These stalls would have originally been open-fronted, as can be seen at a few remaining stalls. However, most were glazed and changed into shops in the 1970s when poultry plucking was banned from the precinct. A few traditional businesses at Leadenhall date back to the late nineteenth century, as do the rich cream and maroon colours in which it is painted.

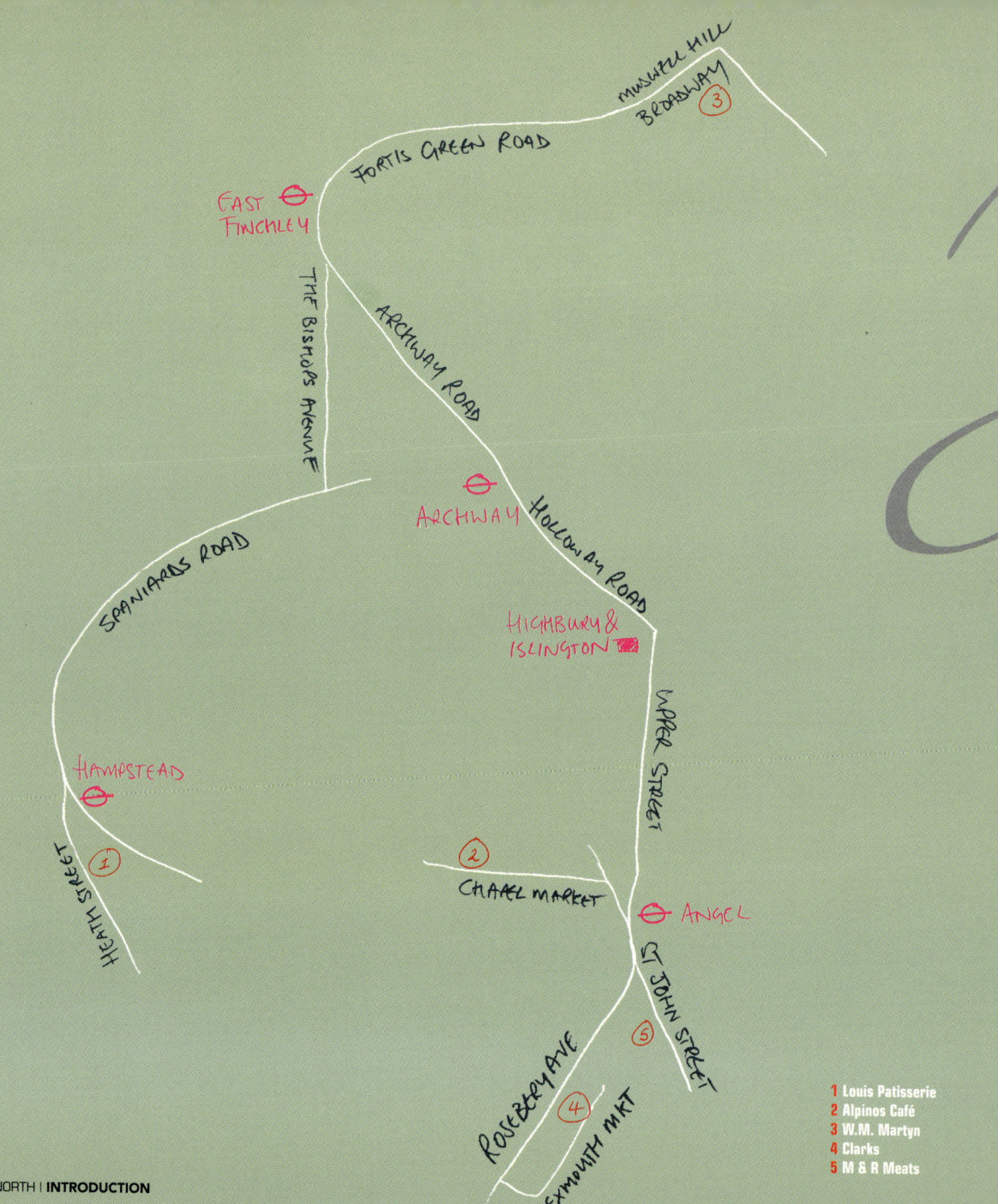

1 Louis Patisserie
2 Alpinos Café
3 W.M. Martyn
4 Clarks
5 M & R Meats

Heading North

ISLINGTON
MUSWELL HILL
HAMPSTEAD

When people talk about North London, they are generally referring to the vast part of the city that lies north of the Marylebone Road.

Up until the nineteenth century, the area was made up of a handful of self-contained villages, which, as London developed and the tube system expanded, gradually became subsumed into the general mass of the city.

Islington was a rural area. In the twelfth century, the monk William Fitz-Stephen portrayed the area as "fields for pasture and open meadows, very pleasant, into which the river's water do flow, and mills are turned about with a delightful noise… beyond them an immense forest extends itself, beautified with woods and groves, and full of the lairs and coverts of wild beasts… and game, stags, bucks, bears and wild bulls".

As the area developed, it became famous for its dairy farms, with the largest farm lying between what is now Liverpool Street and Upper Street.

However, farming declined as London grew, and local farmers turned to manufacturing bricks for the terraces that were springing up all over the city, and by the 1820s, the elegant squares and terraces of Islington had already been built. The latter part of the nineteenth century brought a downturn in fortunes, as the railways brought industrial development and social decline. In the Second World War, Islington suffered significant bomb damage, and entered the post war era in an impoverished state. It was recorded that 'three quarters of its households did not even have running water, an inside lavatory nor a bath'. During the regeneration that followed this period, many of the semi-destroyed Victorian and Georgian terraces were pulled down and housing estates and tower blocks sprang out of the rubble.

In the 1960s there was something of a rediscovery of the area, as the professional classes began to move in, and attempted to preserve the original buildings that remained. Amenities like Camden Passage antiques market were constructed to serve this new population, and new shops and small theatres flourished. However, as late as the 1980s, much of Islington remained run-down, and only in recent years has the area given way to the smart restaurants, galleries and shops that now occupy the streets. Chapel Market, established for some 150 years, remains one of London's famous street markets and is a salutary reminder of Islington's working class roots. The street where the market is now held was first built in 1787 for the residential middle class. It was not until 1868 that the street was used as a market.

Muswell Hill was developed as a suburb of London in Edwardian times, around the turn of the century, and this is reflected in its architecture; substantial, stone dressed, brick-built terraces with ornate plasterwork, served by fine shopping parades and a beautiful Art Deco cinema which has been preserved in its original condition. Bordered on either side by Highgate Woods and Alexandra Park (dominated by the magnificent Alexandra Palace), and having no direct access to rail or tube services, this area very much retains its village feel. It was areas like Muswell Hill, Clapham, Walthamstow and South Kensington that were described as mingled landscapes, where the area was neither town nor country, its inhabitants neither rich nor poor. In his *Tour through England and Wales*, written in 1927, Daniel Defoe notes emergence of "the middle sort of mankind, grown wealthy by trade, and who still taste of London; some live both in the city and the country at the same time". It was in these areas that a hybrid architecture of villas began to emerge, which later came to define London's suburbia.

Hampstead, its name derived from the old English word for homestead, is another village-like niche of London. It was a rural community until the end of the seventeenth century, when it began to be developed as a spa town. These spas could not compete with similar establishments closer to the centre of London, and eventually closed. When the rail lines reached Hampstead in 1860, they brought with them scores of day-trippers to enjoy the Heath, and the popularity of the area grew. Between the years 1871 and 1891, the population of Hampstead doubled, and much of the Hampstead standing today was built in these years.

In 1888, the area of the Heath, previously owned by a wealthy landowner, was handed over to the municipality, and has been protected ever since for public use. Covering over 800 acres, the Heath is one of the most fascinating parklands in London, with woodland, rolling grassland and with its centre piece, Kenwood House, dating back to the seventeenth century.

Hampstead itself remains a very exclusive enclave, home to many established artists, writers and politicians.

Louis Patisserie

32 Heath Street, NW3

Louis Patisserie was founded by Mr and Mrs Louis, when they came to London from Hungary in 1963. The shop window boasts a marvellous array of cakes all baked on-site in the basement ovens according to recipes from Hungary and Poland.

Inside the tearoom, customers are served silver service in cups and saucers, and pastry trays are brought to the table for selection.

The decor is intricate and beautiful with button backed sofas, mahogany panelling and cut glass tables. The patisserie attracts a broad range of clientele and it is a good place to have a relaxing cup of tea and reflect on life.

75

Alpino

97 Chapel Market, N1

Italian immigrants Mr and Mrs Pini opened this coffee shop in 1959, and it has changed hands three times since then. It is currently owned by Simon Cheung who states "most people around here don't like change, so I will keep it just as it is". No bad thing given the striking 1960s design.

The walls are painted cream and the furniture is a mix of dark wood and Formica. The booth style tables and chairs were made bespoke for the cafe in the early 1960s. The table tops are laminated and the seats are hard-wearing red vinyl. The lamp fittings date back to the 1950s. One of the biggest changes is that the first floor that was once Mr and Mrs Pini's home was transformed into a lounge for taxi drivers; this was due to the fact that London Carriage Office is nearby and the taxi drivers used to wait here before their exams. According to Simon, if you jump in a taxi on the other side of London they will know Alpino!

77

W. Martyn

135 Muswell Hill Broadway, N10

This coffee shop in the pretty enclave of Muswell Hill was founded in 1863 by Mr Martyn, who left his family farm in Devon to set up shop. It originally started as general grocery store selling basic household goods, but when coffee and tea brands became more accessible, the emphasis changed and the shop became 'tea and coffee specialists and retailers of fine foods'. Two other stores were opened in Golders Green and Finchley, run by W. Martyn's sons, but they closed when the sons retired in the mid 1950s.

The current owner, William Martyn, the great grandson of the original owner, hopes that the shop will stay in the family, and makes sure that his four year old son comes into the shop regularly. He keeps the shop in traditional ways, and insists "the staff must count the change back into the customers hands as this has always been customer policy".

79

The decor has also been left as was. A traditional wooden counter stretches the length of the shop and goods are piled high on handmade shelves above. The staff serve customers from behind the counter, reaching high on ladders to collect goods from top shelves. An old balance set of scales is prominantly placed, and is still being used today to weigh out nuts, dried fruit and pounds of sugar. Notice the scales have mirrors attached; this was an early day security device.

There is also a separate counter with a small opening, where the goods are paid for. The coffee roaster in the front window roasts all kinds of different coffees throughout the day, filling the shop with a fantastic smell that makes one want to just stay and shop for all the things that you just can't get at a supermarket.

"THE STAFF MUST COUNT THE CHANGE BACK INTO THE CUSTOMERS HANDS AS THIS HAS ALWAYS BEEN CUSTOMER POLICY"

WILLIAM MARTYN, PROPRIETOR

Clarks & Sons

46 Exmouth Market, EC1

Exmouth Market would have once been a street with fruit and vegetable stalls, barbershops, chemists, butchers and fishmongers; today it's a row of brand new cafes and restaurants. Yet snuggled in between, and standing out like a sore thumb is Clarks Pie and Mash shop.

It opened 40 years ago and has not changed since. The seats are high backed wooden benches, the tables have ornate metalwork legs, the lights are a typical 1960s design and the walls are tiled.

On a windy, wet day Pat Clark, who runs the shop with her husband, will whip up a warming home-cooked pie, just perfect comfort food!

83

M & R Meats

399 St John Street, EC1

Set up by butchers Mr Late and Mr Bland in the 1920s, the tiled signage of this shop still reads their names. Although this shop has changed hands a number of times over the years, it is still run as a traditional butchers, and is currently owned by Mr Wilkes and Mr Haggerty. Like their predecessors, they still buy their meat from Smithfield Market at the other end of St John Street, and although they are not open every day, are well worth a visit.

Behind the brown tiled frontage, the interior of this shop is still kept in a traditional style, and although it has been refurbished, it is similar to how it would have been when it was established. The walls are tiled in cream with a simple brown border, and there is a pay station in the corner. The surfaces in the window are marble and there is a light sprinkling of sawdust on the floor. Below the shop is a basement, which is used as it always has been for the storage and preparing of the meat.

85

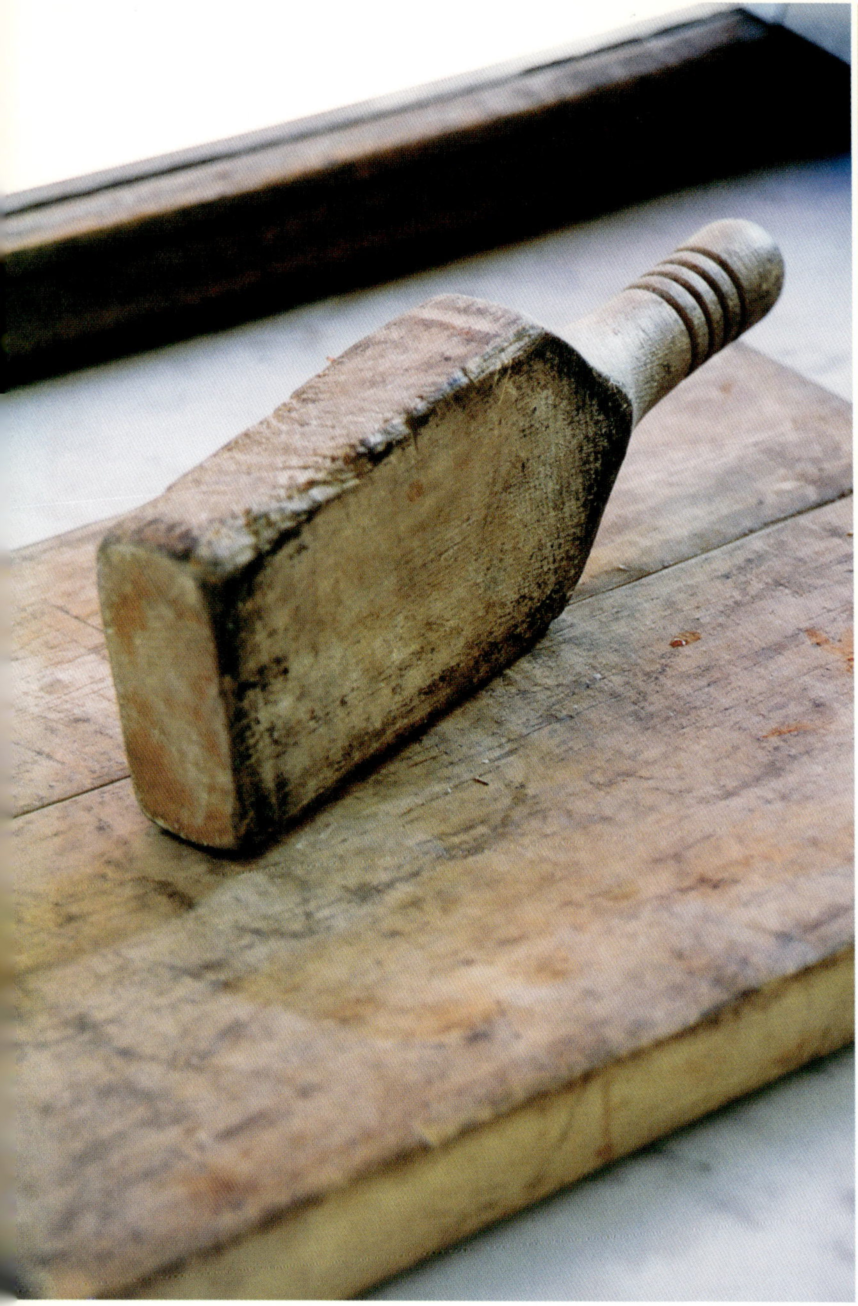
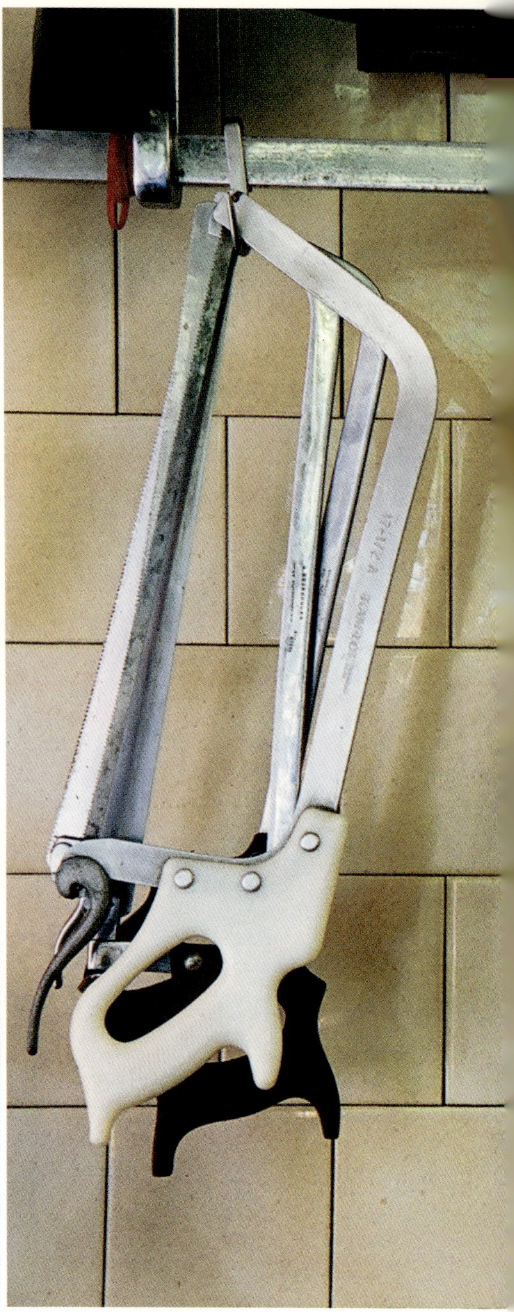

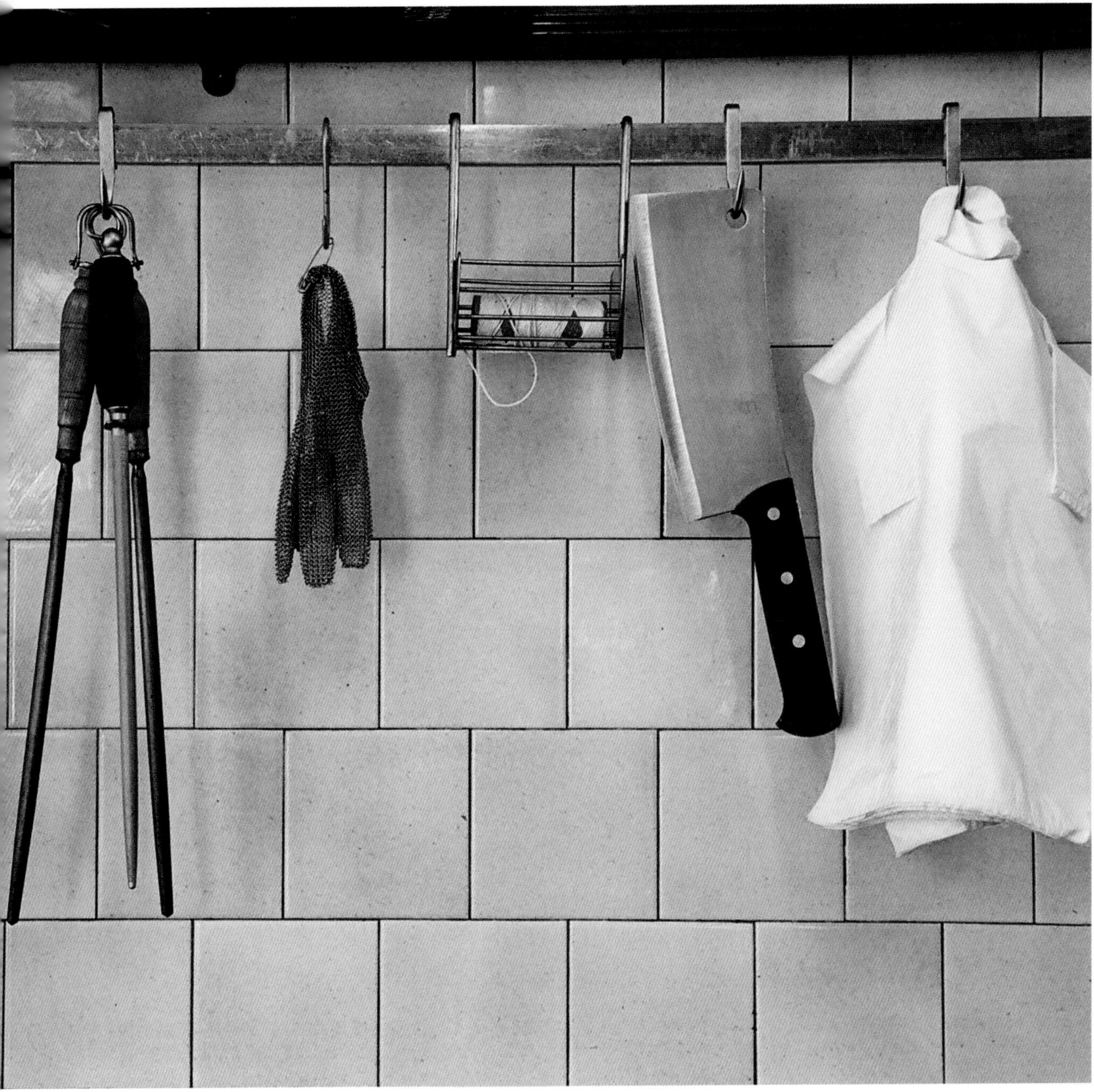

1 Goddards
2 Gambardella
3 R.W. Dring & Co
4 Kennedy's
5 L.S. Mash & Son

88 | SOUTH OF THE RIVER | INTRODUCTION

South of the River

BRIXTON
GREENWICH
DEPTFORD

London, to a degree, is two cities in one; north of the river, and south, both with very individual atmospheres. South London is a dynamic urban sprawl, comprised of lively neighbourhoods and communities, history and traditions. It is impossible to encapsulate the entire sub-city, so this section will focus on three areas; Greenwich, Deptford and Brixton.

Spanning the border of south-east and south-west London, Brixton is one of South London's most vibrant neighbourhoods. It was first recorded in 1067 as 'Brixistane', a north-eastern district of Surrey, its name meaning 'the stone of Brihtsige' (stones were used as the meeting point for communities). It was virtually a wasteland until the beginning of the nineteenth century, when the construction of Vauxhall Bridge provided improved access to Central London, triggering a slow suburban development. Between the 1860s and 90s, railways and trams linked Brixton to the centre of London, and led to a development boom, as people of humble employment sought houses with cheap access to the city. Electric Avenue, the main shopping street running through the area, was so named after it became the first street in the area to be lit by electricity.

Towards the end of the century, the larger, more middle class houses had been converted to lodging houses, which attracted people working in theatres and music halls, marking the start of a close affinity of the area with the arts. In the 1940s and 50s, there was an influx of West Indian immigrants. The first came on the ship *Empire Windrush* and found their way to the area after being housed in Stockwell. These West Indian communities still define the character of Brixton today. It has not all been plain sailing; the riots of the 1980s and 90s and the deep rooted drug problems bear witness to the years of poverty and neglect. However, its richness of cultural influence and vaguely anarchic atmosphere, makes it a colourful, exciting, edgy and unique area.

Greenwich is primarily renowned for Greenwich Meantime, the prime meridian of zero degrees longitude passing through the famous Greenwich Observatory. It is one of South London's major tourist destinations; with its pretty winding streets, and quaint, diminutive architecture, it feels like a maritime village that accidentally found itself attached to the tail end of a metropolis.

The name Greenwich derives from the Saxon word for 'Green Village', and the area has a rich history, with close affiliation to royalty. The first palace to be built in the area was in the thirteenth century during the time of King Edward I. Through to the days of the Tudors, some form of royal presence had its base in the area. The palace was destroyed in the seventeenth century, during the civil war, and Charles II decided to rebuild it, but ran out of funds after completion of just one wing, which now houses the Royal Naval College.

The area's ports and docks were the source of Greenwich's development during the nineteenth century, with shipbuilding a common trade amongst its residents. The *Cutty Sark*, still docked near the Naval College, was one of the famous tea clippers that sailed the globe at the end of the century. The docks continued to thrive until the Second World War, after which they began to suffer. The last London dock closed in 1981.

With the pretty Nash style terraces dating from the 1830s, and its many antiques and nautical nick-nack shops, the area is a lovely one to walk around. The covered market still boasts the Victorian inscription on one of its arches: 'A false balance is an abomination to the Lord but a weight is his delight'.

Near to Greenwich, but very much distinct, Deptford's name comes from the 'deep ford' across the old River Ravensbourne. Henry VIII was responsible for much of the development of this area, by bringing his navy to its docks in 1513. Many famous ships were built and equipped in the Royal Dockyards, and the district developed in this way through until the eighteenth century. Although some remnants of this history has survived, much of Deptford has a reputation for being down-at-heel. This is slowly changing, as development funding is ploughed into the area. With new buildings, such as the remarkable Laban dance centre, and its proximity to Goldsmith's College, it is being heralded as 'the new Shoreditch' in honour of its happening artistic and music scene.

Goddards
203 Deptford High Street, SE8

This cosy pie shop has been in the Goddard family since 1890. First based in nearby Evelyn Street, the shop was forced to move to its current location by the council, who wanted to redevelop the site (the original building has remained derelict since they moved out in the mid 1960s).

Its current owner, Clive, took over from his grandfather, George, and his daughter, granddaughter and grandson, work alongside him. It is said of George that he worked in the shop every day of his adult life until his retirement only two years prior to his death, at the age of 89.

In the early days, Goddard's supplied pubs with pies, pickled gherkins, pickled eggs and even crisps, which were fried in the upstairs kitchens and packaged together with a little blue bag of salt. Today the shop is renowned for having pie-eating competitions, the record being five dozen plates of two pies with mash!

The pews are almost 200 years old, but were bought 20 years ago from an old Methodist church. White topped tables sit on a wide planked wooden floor and the walls are decorated with historic pictures of trains and ships local to the area. This pie shop is definitely worth the visit, preferably on a cold day, so that you can warm yourself with a pie and cup of builder's tea.

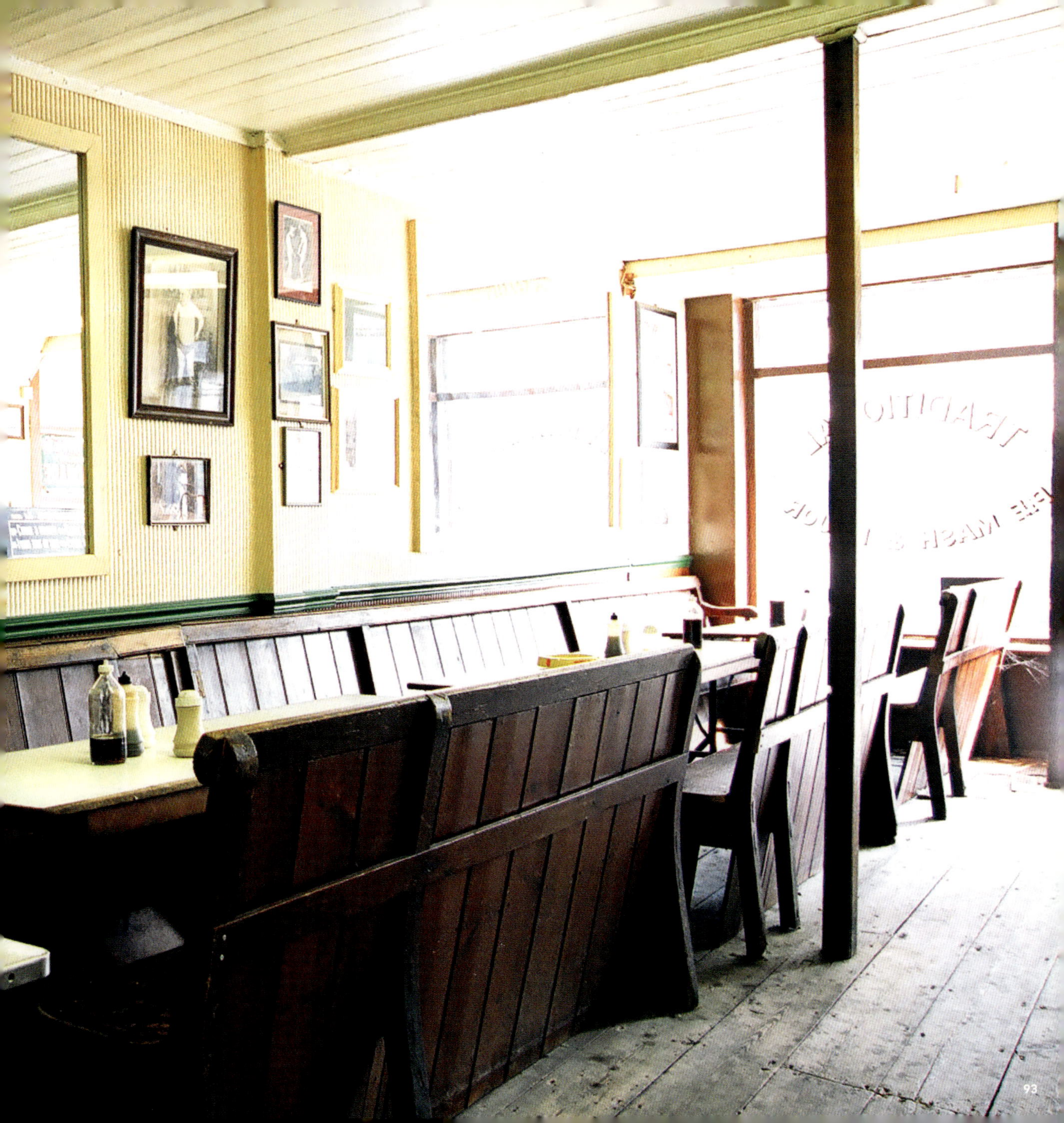

Gambardella

47/48 Vanbrugh Park, SE3

Mr Gambardella, the founder of this vibrantly colourful cafe, moved to London from Naples in the 1920s and started out running a barbershop in Stepney. He made the move south of the river and into catering in 1927, opening this cafe and a sweetshop next door. Both shops ran successfully until five years ago when it was decided to extend the cafe by knocking through to the sweetshop.

Mr Gambardella worked in the cafe until his retirement at the age of 80. His 70 year old wife now runs the place along with his two nephews, James and Alex.

The 1950s style fixtures and fittings were taken from an old Lyon's tea house. The walls are mock marble with chrome trims, and the laminate tables, walls and chairs are dazzlingly orange.

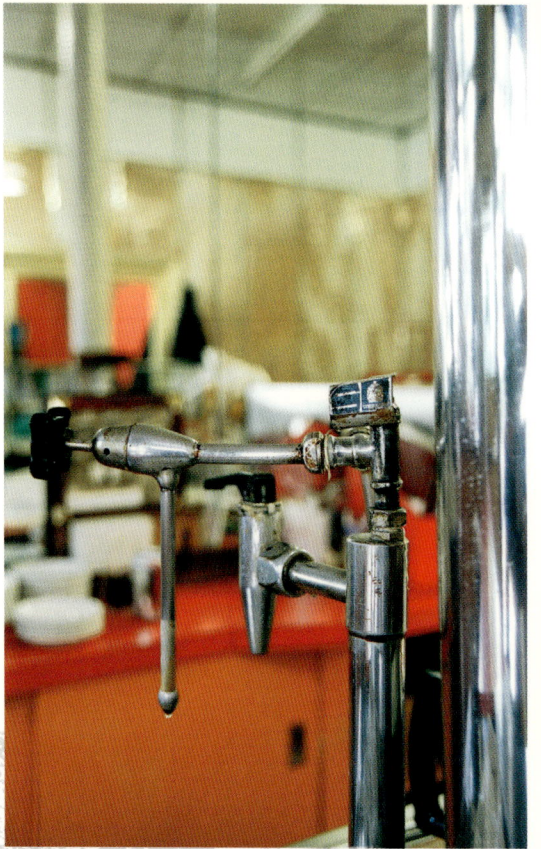

MBARDELLA Refreshments

R.W. Dring & Co
22 Royal Hill, SE10

This friendly local butchers is the last vestige of what used to be a bustling village style high street. Established in 1964, it is now run by the founders' sons, Bob and Dave Dring. Bob says: "On this short parade, there used to be a grocers, a fruit and vegetable shop and a fishmongers. It was all you would ever want in one street – just like a mini supermarket!" There is virtually nothing of that left now. The building next door, which dates from the 1690s, has been left derelict for the past 11 years, but R.W. Dring continues to do a roaring trade. Each Christmas the queue for turkeys wraps right around the block.

The interior is totally untouched since the day it opened. The pastel 1960s style clock still ticks away on the wall, sawdust is scattered on the floor and the same well-worn butcher's block is being used to cut the meat.

PORK

Kennedy's

**64-66 Deptford High St, Deptford, SE8
and 10 Denmark Hill, SE5**

Kennedy's in Deptford is part of a chain that has been selling meat and provisions in shops all over south-east London since 1877. The shop in Peckham Rye has now closed; however, the branches in Camberwell, Bromley and this one in Deptford have managed to survive. Mr Hogan, who is the owner of all three Kennedy's shops, proudly states, "This is the oldest shop left on Deptford high street".

Similar to other butchers, the walls are covered in cream tiles with green borders and mirrors and pictures displayed randomly. A large counter dominates the shop, behind which marble surface tops and wooden shelving are stacked high with tins of pease pudding and baked beans.

Although it now seems a bit run down, this butchers still proves very popular, and people come from miles around to buy here.

Butchers

The decor of a traditional London butchers is fairly uniform, and dates back to Victorian times. Tiles (either decorated or plain white or cream with a green or brown border), were used to keep the shop cool and easy to clean. Counters and sideboards were topped with marble slabs to keep meat fresh and uncontaminated, and a sprinkling of sawdust would have been thrown on the floor to soak up blood and moisture. The traditional butchers' uniform was a blue and white striped apron over a white overcoat and a straw hat. The shop would have been open-fronted, displaying the meat on tiered counters or from hooks outside the shop. Today they have all been glassed in to comply with health and safety regulations.

As in the past, much of the meat in today's London butchers is sourced at Smithfield Market in Clerkenwell, which has been dealing in meat and livestock for over 800 years, making it one of the oldest markets in London. Smithfield is a remarkable, Grade II listed building in itself, and although the interior has been thoroughly renovated to comply with modern hygiene standards, the exterior remains strikingly elegant and is, as they say, well worth a butchers.

"THIS IS THE OLDEST SHOP LEFT ON DEPTFORD HIGH STREET" MR HOGAN, PROPRIETOR

L.S. Mash & Sons

11 Atlantic Road, Brixton, SW9

This fishmongers was opened under the railway arches of Brixton station in 1934 by one Mr Mills. When he died, he left it to his protégé, Lorne Mash, who started work in the shop at the age of 14. At one time the shop had 22 members of staff. Today there are only two – Lorne and his half brother (otherwise known as the 'Mitchell Brothers' for their resemblance to characters in the soap opera *Eastenders*). Its decor is simple and traditional – white and green tiles with decorative inserts of fishermen and fishing scenes. It is the last shop left in the railway arches. At the top of the arch, a metal grill is adorned with bright green metal fish.

L.S. Mash is known to be the first fresh fishmongers in South London, and continues to stock a broad range of seafood, which they buy from Billingsgate Market in East London. In Lorne's words, "it's a hard life, but a good life. It keeps you going".

"A HARD LIFE, BUT A GOOD LIFE. IT KEEPS YOU GOING"

LORNE MASH, PROPRIETOR

102 | EAST END | **INTRODUCTION**

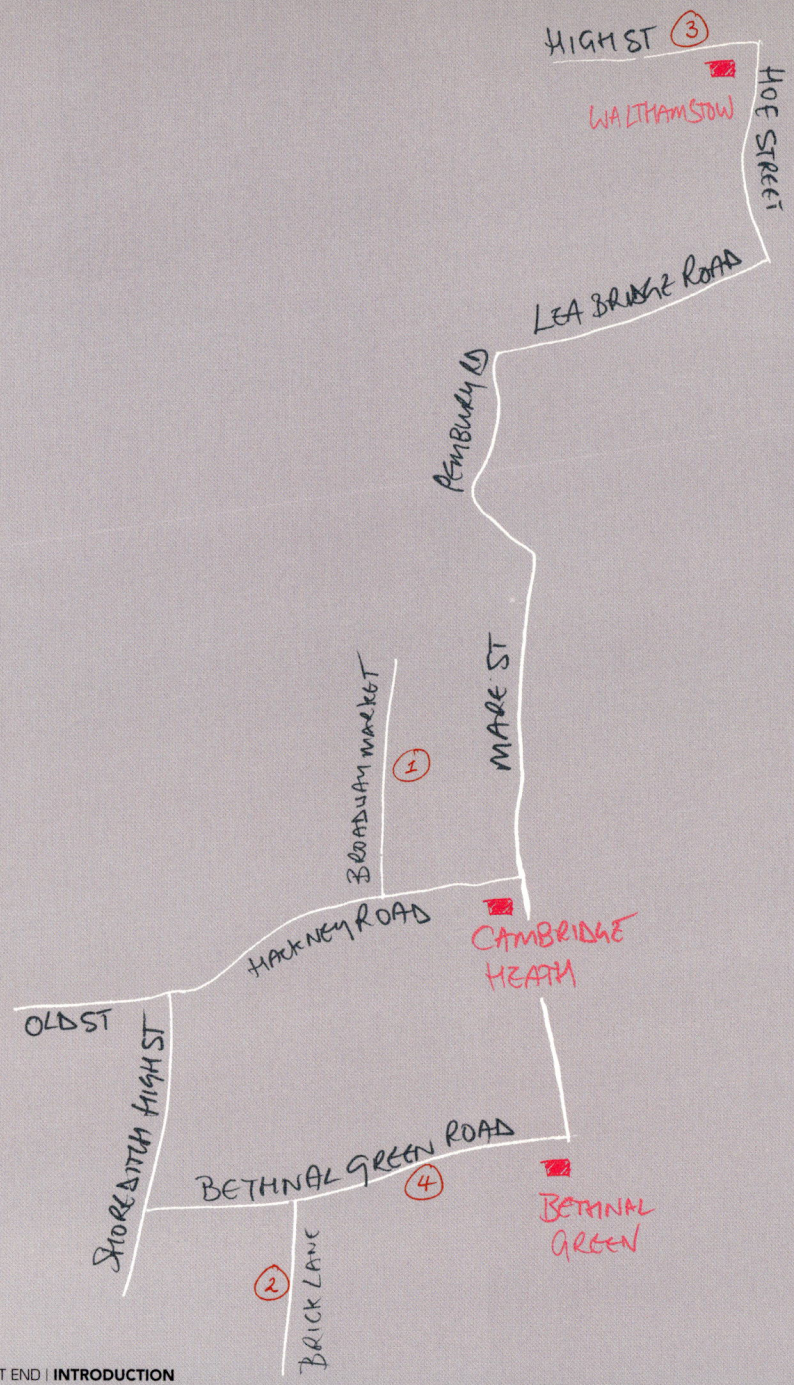

1 F. Cooke
2 Beigel Bake
3 L. Manze
4 E. Pellicci

EAST END

BRICK LANE
BETHNAL GREEN
WALTHAMSTOW

The East End of London is a vaguely delineated area north of the river, stretching approximately from Whitechapel, at the edge of the City, through Bethnal Green, Mile End, Hackney and Bow down to Canary Wharf and the Docklands. Its romanticised history of cockneys and gangsters symbolises the toughness of the British spirit in the face of adversity, and provides a glossy veneer for an area long racked by poverty and crime.

The misfortunes of London's East End date back to the early seventeenth century, when the unpleasant trades of London – slaughter houses, fish farms and breweries, were located in the area – as the dominant west winds meant that the rest of London was kept odour free.

The area developed with these industries and through the maritime trade, where casual labour was relied upon, thus attracting large immigrant populations. These populations have shifted and changed over the years, each one leaving its mark on the area. The East End, more than any other part of London, has been defined and built by immigrants from all nationalities and ethnicities – Huguenots, Jews, Turkish communities, Bangladeshis, Africans and many more have come here and made the area their own.

Through the nineteenth century, industry developed alongside the docks, and so did the housing to accommodate their labour force. The tightly packed streets quickly deteriorated into slums. In the latter half of the nineteenth century, attempts were made to remedy this situation, through the establishment of the Peabody Trust, Barnardo's Children's home and the Salvation Army, but given the magnitude of the problems, they could not provide much more than minor alleviation. Crime grew alongside poverty, and even today crime rates remain relatively high, with part of Hackney still known as the 'murder-mile'.

During the Second World War, the East End was one of the areas worst affected by the bombs (being the centre of London's industry and maritime trade, it was an obvious target). The post war reconstruction left a legacy of vast housing estates and tower blocks, bringing a new definition to the area. Ship containerisation caused the docks to close in 1969 resulting in a high level of unemployment.

Nowadays, the East End is still one of London's poorest areas but it is undergoing extensive regeneration, with many of the more unsightly tower blocks pulled down or renovated. The proximity of some of the areas to the City means they have become more desirable and are slowly being gentrified, and the recent success of London's bid for the 2012 Olympics, to be hosted throughout the East End, means that this process will surely spread eastwards.

The area of Brick Lane and Spitalfields is most certainly on the up. Nestled between Bethnal Green and Liverpool Street, it is renowned for providing a haven for those fleeing from persecution. In the early eighteenth century, the area was settled by Huguenots, escaping religious hatred in France. In the nineteenth century, Jews fleeing the pogroms in Eastern Europe arrived *en masse*, and then in the middle of the twentieth century, a large Bangladeshi community found its way to Brick Lane, and is the dominant presence there today. Alongside this bustling Asian community, in the higgledy piggledy Georgian terraces around Spitalfields, affluent media-bods and designers have taken over. On Sundays, the discrepancies between the different inhabitants of the area are accentuated by the various markets: Brick Lane boasts a hectic market full of everything from one pound t-shirts to stolen bikes, and Petticoat Lane, around the corner, sells knock-off electrical goods, whilst Spitalfields attends to the needs of the fashion conscious, with funky stalls by up-and-coming designers.

Just a few hundred metres north-east of Brick Lane lies Bethnal Green, a much poorer, more mixed community than its upwardly mobile neighbour. Historically, this area housed some of the worst of the East End slums. To this day, on Lambs Gardens you can see the tiny terraces that used to be garden sheds, converted for human inhabitancy. This area, and adjacent Whitechapel, was Jack the Ripper's notorious haunt, and later was the homeland of Ronnie and Reggie Kray's gangland rule. Today, whilst still not exactly illustrious, Bethnal Green is home to an eclectic mix of students, artists, Pakistani and Bangladeshi communities and young families, making it a vibrant, bustling area, well worth a visit.

Walthamstow, at the northern end of the Victoria Line, derives its name from Weald – forest, Ham – home, Stow – place. It has always been an important crossing point on the River Lea, and developed through the middle ages, growing rapidly during the second half of the nineteenth century, along with so much of London. Walthamstow Village still bears witness to its medieval past, with sixteenth century almshouses, timbered Tudor buildings and a church dating back to the Middle Ages.

F. Cooke

9 Broadway Market, E8

The Cooke family have been supplying Londoners with eels, pie and mash since 1865, and were, at one time, one of London's foremost eel wholesalers, with shops not only in Hackney but also in Bermondsey, Hoxton and Clerkenwell. Today only this one and the one in Hoxton survive, both still run by members of the Cooke family.

Each of Cooke's shops would have been decorated in a similar manner to this one in Broadway Market; the walls covered in white tiles with a green border, sawdust floors, marble tabletops and wooden pew-like benches. The windows in the front of the shop were designed to allow passers-by to buy pies and eels from the street. The eels were stored in specially made metal trays, and could be bought live or served alongside pie and mash. Bob Cooke, who runs the shop, says: "I will probably work here till I drop – I can't see myself retiring, I enjoy it too much."

THIS DISCLOSURE WAS MADE IN THE MEDICAL RESEARCH COUNCILS REPORT FOR 1926-7 ISSUED FEB 24TH 1928

We now have a striking confirmation the medieval notion that **EELS** *have high dietetic value*

INDEED THE BODY OIL IN EELS WHICH IS ALMOST 30% OF THEIR WHOLE SUBSTANCE CONTAINS NOT ONLY VITAMEN "D" – BUT ALMOST AS MUCH VITAMEN "A" AS GOOD COD LIVER OIL

EAT MORE EELS

"I WILL PROBABLY WORK HERE TILL I DROP – I CAN'T SEE MYSELF RETIRING, I ENJOY IT TOO MUCH"

ROBERT COOKE, PROPRIETOR

Beigel Bake

159 Brick Lane, E1

This Jewish bakery has been going strong since 1855, when it was set up in the next door premises. Its popularity meant that it had to move to its current, larger location 26 years ago, where it has stayed unchanged ever since. It is open 24 hours a day, and in the words of long time employee, Joanne Latimer: "taxi drivers, clubbers, local girls and transvestites, you name them we get them!"

In the early days, the bakery only sold bagels with cream cheese and smoked salmon and cheesecake to follow. Later on, other breads, pastries, platzels and chola bread were introduced, as well as the infamous salt beef. This is one of the last vestiges of the Jewish East End, and it stands incongruously amongst the primarily Bangladeshi shops of Brick Lane.

> "TAXI DRIVERS, CLUBBERS, LOCAL GIRLS AND TRANSVESTITES, YOU NAME THEM, WE GET THEM!" — JOANNE LATIMER, EMPLOYEE

109

L. Manze

76 Walthamstow High Street, E17

The great L. Manze has been on Walthamstow high street since 1927. The original owner, Lugis Manze, an Italian immigrant from Ravello, opened five shops, one for each of his sons, but only two remain, this one in Walthamstow and the other in Chapel Market, Islington. The shop has changed hands since then and the current owner, Jackie Cooper, learned her trade from a long-time employee called Millie Casey, who worked at the pie shop from the age of 13 until her retirement at the age of 69. Jackie's brother Tim now runs the Islington branch. Jackie explains: "Nothing has changed since the day it started, the recipes or the interior".

The interior is indeed striking, with high benched booth seating, decorative tiles lining the walls and pendant lights hanging from the anaglypta ceiling. The marble counter can still be seen where once the window would have been open and live eels would have been sold to take away. Today the eels are sold either jellied or stewed, either way considered a gastronomic delight and well worth a try!

Pie and Mash Shops

In Victorian times, a 'take-away' meal would mean buying a pie from one of the 600 pie men that sold their wares on the streets of London. Traditionally the pie man would wake up early and row over to the boats moored on the Thames where he would buy the eels directly from the fishermen. He would then rush home, bake the pies and sell them hot off the tray with vinegar flavouring or pea and parsley sauce; a hot affordable meal for the working class.

In 1850 the first pie and mash shop opened, and many others followed suit. Most pie and mash shops were located near markets, bringing business from both the vendors and their customers. In the early days, the shops had stalls outside that sold live eels for families to take home and cook. This tradition stopped when the economics of keeping live eels (which need to be kept in running water) proved too expensive.

Throughout the Second World War, when food was rationed, the pie and mash shop supplied nutritional food at low cost. Business thrived until the mid 1950s when a swift price increase in rent saw the closure of many factories resulting in a loss of trade from factory workers. Supermarkets opened and convenience foods gradually became more widely available. Consequently most of the pie and mash shops have slowly disappeared.

E. Pellicci

332 Bethnal Green Road, E2

This cafe has been put forward by English Heritage inspectors for a Grade II listing, with the following description: "stylish shop front of custard Vitrolite panels, steel frame and lettering as well as a rich Deco-style marquetry panelled interior, altogether representing an architecturally strong and increasingly rare example of intact and stylish Italian cafe that flourished in London in the inter-war years".

Opened in 1900 by the eponymous Pellicci family from Tuscany, it has been handed down through the family, and is now run by Nevio Pellicci (Nev to his friends and regulars). The impressive decor described above was the initiative of Nevio's mother, Eilde Pellicci, who supervised the construction in 1946. The Art Deco style marquetry was made by one of the best known carpenters at the time, Archille Capocci, whose sample plaque reading 'EP' can still be seen today in place of honour behind the counter.

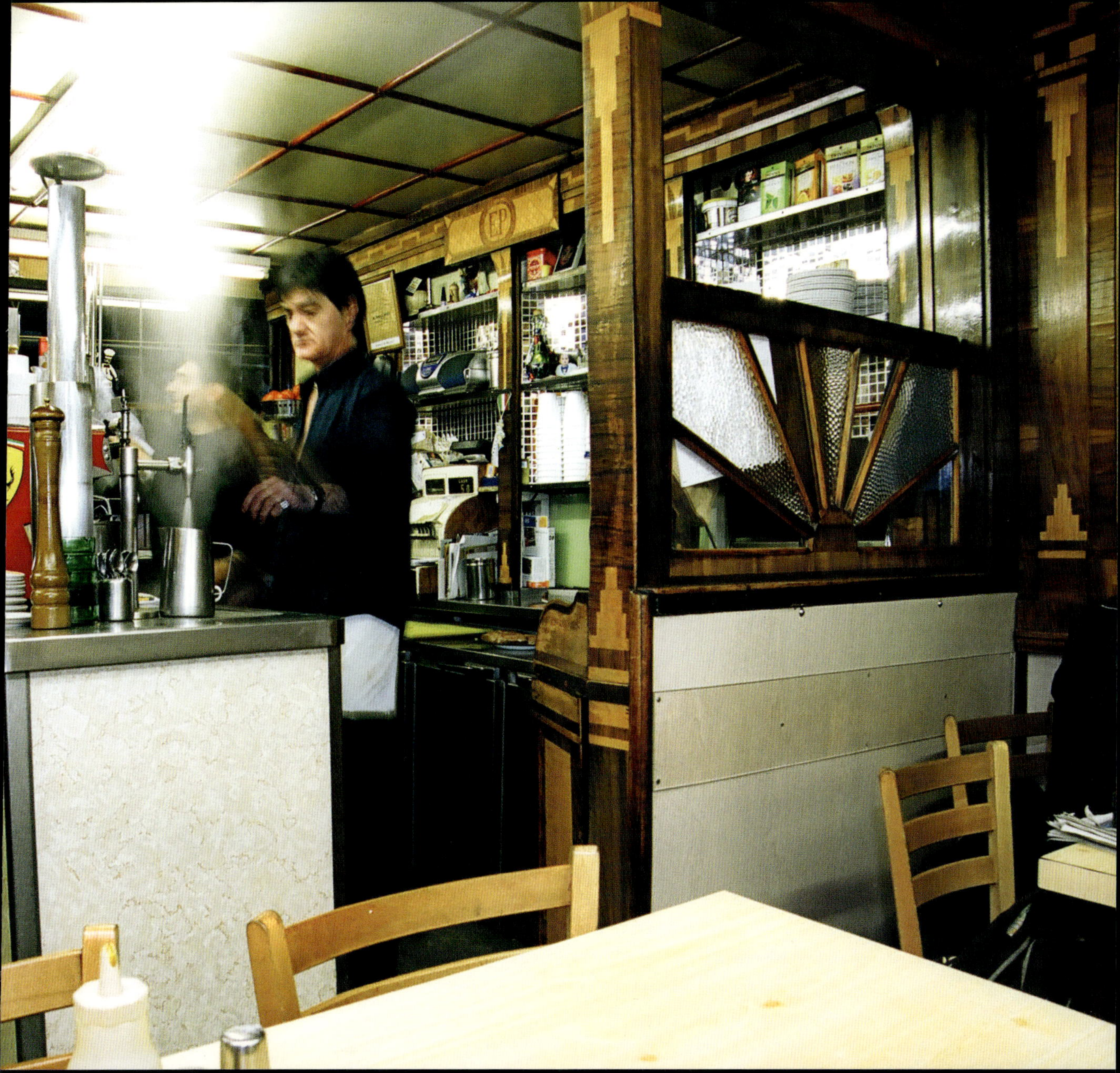

Pellicci's holds a special place in popular culture, and is renonwned for being the local hangout of the notorious Kray twins, East End ganglords of the 1960s, who lived just around the corner in Voss Street. Nevio remembers the Krays vividly and describes them as "true gentlemen, respectful and charming". More recent celebrity diners can be found documented in an autograph book, which sports the signatures of artists, writers and musicians, including Robbie Williams and Oasis.

Nevio is now pushing 80, and his children and grandchildren are eager to learn the business, so they can take over when he finally decides to retire. Nevio Junior, his sister, Anna, and his cousins can be seen waiting tables and memorising orders. Every year in August, the cafe is closed for a month, whilst the family returns to their roots in Tuscany. By the end of the month, though, Nevio is always restless to get back to his espresso machine. Nevio Junior says "he runs around faster than the rest of us!"

"HE RUNS AROUND FASTER THAN THE REST OF US!"
NEVIO JUNIOR ABOUT HIS FATHER

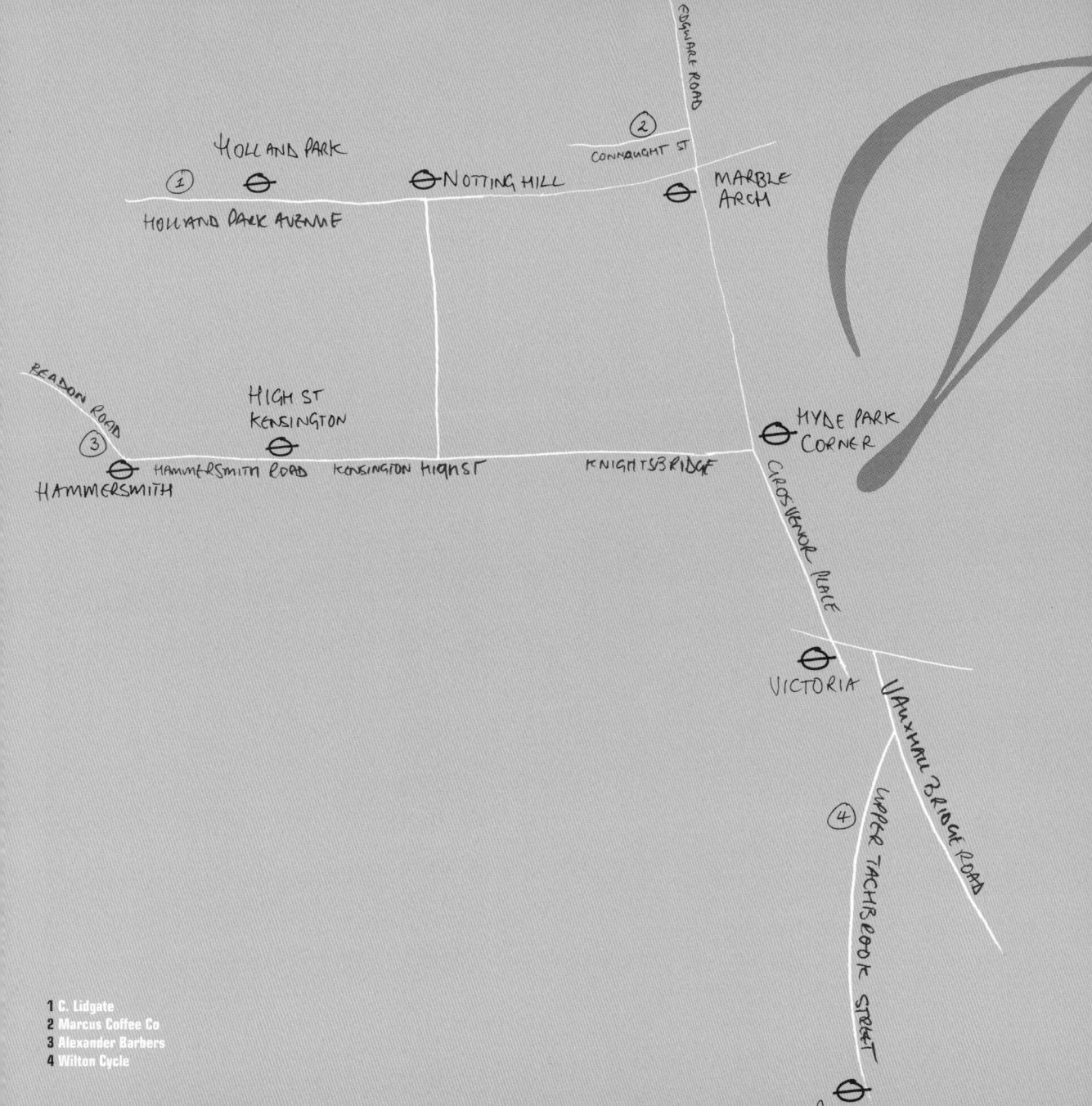

1 **C. Lidgate**
2 **Marcus Coffee Co**
3 **Alexander Barbers**
4 **Wilton Cycle**

WESTWARD BOUND

KNIGHTSBRIDGE
BAYSWATER
WESTBOURNE GROVE
NOTTING HILL
HAMMERSMITH

With the immaculate terraces of Chelsea and Belgravia and the manicured green spaces of Hyde Park and Kensington gardens, much of West London has a genteel grandeur that is subtly distinct from other areas in London, and it has been in vogue ever since royalty moved to Kensington Palace in the late seventh century. However, there is another side to West London, and amongst the trendy cafes and designer clothes shops of Notting Hill, you can sense the rich multicultural history that has reached even this glossy part of the city.

Knightsbridge, after Oxford Street, is probably the best-known shopping district of London. Harrods, a former East End grocer, is now one of London's largest and most popular department stores, occupying a magnificent Art Nouveau palace, and offering services including piano tuning and dog coat fitting. Just down the road, in Sloane Street, the luxury goods of the world are on offer – provided you have the cash to pay for them.

Bayswater has a more diverse population. This is the area south-west of Paddington which runs from Bayswater Road northward to Bishops Bridge Road and west to Westbourne Grove. The name has been in use since the mid seventeenth century, and refers to 'Bayard's watering place' – a watering hole for horses, known to have been in existence as early as 1380.

The area, once rural, was heavily developed throughout the late eighteenth and early nineteenth centuries. It was one of the first suburbs to be colonised by wealthy Londoners moving west to escape the increasing squalor of city life, and was known as a fashionable district. Due to commercialisation around Paddington, it gradually declined and it is now a very mixed area, with pockets of opulence around Hyde Park and along the Western ends of it, and a large second generation immigrant population – primarily Greek and Arab – in the less affluent north.

Westbourne Grove was Bayswater's first major shopping street. William Whiteley's shop at number 43 was opened in 1863 to cater for every need 'from a pin to an elephant at short notice'. It grew at a pace, taking over 15 neighbouring premises, and alarming local merchants to such a degree that when Whiteley opened his meat counter in 1876, local butchers burned effigies of him on Guy Fawkes night. He died at the hand of his estranged son in 1907, and the shop moved away from Westbourne Grove.

Notting Hill is one of the more interesting, cosmopolitan areas of West London. The area developed, as did so much of London, in the nineteenth century, as an area of shops and markets serving the large houses on the estates and terraces of the surrounding areas. Prior to that its only renown had been as 'gravel pits at the end of Church Street'. By the end of the nineteenth century, the area had become primarily working class, with landlords buying up little terraces and renting out rooms to the poor, and during Victorian times, its streets and alleys were deemed 'worse than the East End'.

As a poor area, it naturally attracted an immigrant population and after the Second World War, West Indian immigrants started to arrive. The friction between these newcomers and the indigenous white working class population culminated in the Notting Hill race riots of 1958. By the mid 60s, the situation had improved, as community leaders worked to ease the tensions. Around this time artists started to arrive; writers, actors, rock stars and designers made the area their own, giving it a reputation as a hub of bohemian creativity; one that it still enjoys today. The Caribbean influence can still be felt, particularly during the Notting Hill Carnival, held in August each year; however, the popularity of the area means that many parts have priced out all but the wealthiest.

Hammersmith is London's gateway to the west. The area began as an isolated village where the willows by the river supported a trade in basket making, and it grew into a flourishing riverside suburb. Gradual commercialisation compromised the tranquility of the area, and when the fly-over was built in the 1960s, most of the area was cut off from the river, and became a busy traffic intersection. Hammersmith today is a mixed area – much of it is ugly concrete and congested roads, but other parts are much more pleasant, particularly the stretch along the river, which is lovely to walk along on a summers' afternoon.

C. Lidgate

110 Holland Park Avenue, W11

David Lidgate is the fourth generation of his family to run this 150 year old butchers, and his son, Danny, is already set to follow family traditions. The shop today is very much as it was when it first opened. Remarkably, the shop front is still in almost perfect condition, with its eye-catching pilaster stretching the width of the building. The layout hasn't changed much either, and although the fittings are new or refurbished, they are still very much in keeping with tradition.

   David and Danny maintain the establishment as a top rate butchers (a series of awards take pride of place on the shop walls), and they regularly visit the select farms and estates that supply their free range and organic meat, to inspect feed, breed and environment.

GATE

Marcus Coffee Co
13 Connaught Street, W2

Hungarian immigrants, Mr and Mrs Markus, established this business 49 years ago, and both worked in the shop until their deaths.

This wonderful shop is a pleasure to visit; the aroma of fresh coffee fills the air, wafting up from the sacks of coffee beans resting on the floor waiting to be roasted, ground and packed. In the middle of the shop stands an antiquated packing machine, so old it is impossible to get parts for it any more. The only man who knows how to fix it is based in Germany, and has to fly out especially when it breaks down.

"WE ROAST THE COFFEE ON THE PREMISES EACH DAY. YOU CAN'T GET FRESHER THAN THAT"
MOHAMMAD SARWAR, PROPRIETOR

Alexander Barbers

3-4 Metropolitan Station Buildings, W6

This barbershop has been at this site since 1911, and has changed hands numerous times. It was taken over 30 years ago by the Pavlou family, who have kept it much as it was.

It is light and airy with entrance doors on both sides, one opening to the Hammersmith station side and the other coming in from the street.

Heavy white porcelain basins are lined up opposite white steel and chrome barber chairs. The black leather upholstery is on its last legs, and has to be taped together to keep it from falling apart. A wall cabinet houses some interesting artefacts and barbers' tools from bygone days. A towel steamer sits unused in the corner, evidence that the days of wet shaves and singeing been and gone.

PRICE LIST
HAIRCUT FROM 8.50
LONG HAIR 9.00
WAS CUT & DRY 11.00
LONGHAIR WET CUT 12.00
SHAVE 8.00
HOT TOWEL 1.00
BEARD TRIM 3.00
FACE MASSAGE 7.00
CHILDREN UNDER 8 6.50
MONDAY TO FRIDAY
SENIOR CITIZEN 5.00
MONDAY TO THURSDAY
MON TO SAT 7AM 6PM
FRIDAY TILL 7PM

BARBER SHOP

3

Vaseline
TRADE MARK
SHAMPOO
Leaves YOUR HAIR
SO EASY TO SET

Wiltons Cycles & Wireless Co

28 Upper Tachbrook Street, SW1

This fun, specialist shop first opened in 1895 on Wilton Road, just around the corner, and has been at its current premises since 1935.

Robert Head is the proprietor of the shop, which he inherited from his parents, who took it over in the 1930s. Robert has run the shop since the 1970s, and he has lived in the flat above most of his life.

Wiltons started out by supplying parts for the motor industry, but as time went on it diversified to the wireless or radio and then to bicycles. Today it mostly specialises in collector's model toys. It is a shop well worth visiting; it may not be there for long, as Robert plans to retire soon!

"WHEN THE RADIO DIED OUT WE HAD TO DIVERSIFY"
ROBERT HEAD, PROPRIETOR

126 | WESTWARD BOUND | WILTONS CYCLES & WIRELESS Co

CLOSED
FOR LUNCH
OPEN
2-30

CLOSED
HALF DAY
THURSDAY
AFTERNOON

BACK IN A
FEW
MINUTES

ABINGDON
KING DICK
SPANNER
Webley
AIR RIFLES

Webley

127

Acknowledgements

Many thanks to all the shops we visited, those that have been included as well as those that we unfortunately could not feature due to lack of space. We appreciate all your help and encouragement.

Many thanks also to the following family, friends and colleagues for their support, help and input: Margaret Venables, Simon Gow, Bernadette Roberts, Jo Lal, Emma Cragie, Quentin Koetter, Steve Benson, Mr Le Guo and all the team at Snappy Snaps in Greenwich, London, SE10. Thanks to Catherine Grant, who commissioned this publication. Also thanks to Alex Franklin for the use of his photography of T. Fox & Co (pp. 62–63).

Selected Bibliography

– Tally Abecassis & Claudine Sauve, *Barbershops*, London: Black Dog Publishing, 2005
– Ackroyd, Peter, *London The Biography*, London: Vintage, 2001
– Draper-Stumm, Tara and Derk Kendall, *London's Shops the World's Emporium* London: English Heritage, 2002
– *The Essential Guide to London's Best Food Shops*, London: New Holland, 2000
– Glinert, Ed, *The London Compendium, A Street-by-Street Exploration of The Hidden Metropolis*, London: Penguin Books, 2004
– Heathcote, Edwin, *London Caffs*, London: Wiley-Academy, 2004
– *London Food Shops 2002/03*, London: Harden's, 2002
– Maddox, Adrian, *Classic Cafes*, London: Black Dog Publishing, 2003
– *The Rough Guide to London*, London, New York: Rough Guides, 2003
– *Shopping in London*, Insight Guides, 2002
– *StyleCity London*, Thames & Hudson, 2005
– Weinreb, Ben and Christopher Hibbert, *The London Encyclopaedia*, London: Macmillan, 2005

Articles

– Kelly, Jon, "Closed All Hours", *Daily Mirror*, 28 January 2004
– Lamont, Tom "The Last Cuppa?", *Time Out London*, 18 August 2004
– Low, Valentine "Era Ends as Soho Café Pays Price of Rent Rises", *Evening Standard*, 3 August 2004
– Sanchez, Matheus "My Café is a Film Star", *Evening Standard*, 24 June 2005
– Smith, David "Greasy Spoon Caffs Are Crushed by Coffee Giants", *The Observer*, 1 August 2004
– Stanley, Bob "The Real Caffeine hit", *The Times*, 10 October 2003
– Sweet, Matthew "Keep the Change", *The Independent On Sunday*, 15 June 2003

Black Dog Publishing
Architecture Art Design Fashion History Photography Theory and Things

© 2006 Black Dog Publishing Limited, the artists and authors
All rights reserved

Text by Sally Venables
Photography by Brian Benson
Design by Steve Williams
Edited by Cigalle Hanaor

Black Dog Publishing Limited
Unit 4.4 Tea Building
56 Shoreditch High Street
London E1 6JJ
Tel: +44 (0)20 7613 1922
Fax: +44 (0)20 7613 1944
Email: info@bdp.demon.co.uk
www.bdpworld.com

All opinions expressed within this publication are those of the authors and not necessarily of the publisher.

British Library Cataloguing-in-Publication Data.

A CIP record for this book is available from the British Library.

ISBN 1 904772 44 7

All rights reserved. No part of this publication may be reproduced, stored in a retrieval system, or transmitted, in any form or by any means, electronic, mechanical, photocopying, recording, or otherwise, without prior permission of the publisher.

Every effort has been made to trace the copyright holders, but if any have been inadvertently overlooked the publishers will be pleased to make the necessary arrangements at the first opportunity.